GHOSTS OF NORTHWESTERN NEW JERSEY

GHOSTS OF NORTHWESTERN NEW JERSEY

ROBERT OAKES

HAUNTED AMERICA

Published by Haunted America
A Division of The History Press
Charleston, SC
www.historypress.com

First published 2022

Manufactured in the United States

ISBN 9781467150026

Library of Congress Control Number: 2022937940

CONTENTS

ACKNOWLEDGEMENTS

I would like to thank and acknowledge Henry Charlton Beck; Mark Sceurman and Mark Moran of *Weird NJ*; L'Aura Hladik; Lynda Lee Macken; Edith Wharton; Cindy Barton; Ren Giliberti; Matthew Beland and Drew University; Bill Kroth, Ken D., Doug Francisco and the Sterling Hill Mining Museum; Carl Zipper, George Pantos and the Mount Allamuchy Scout Reservation; the Lake Hopatcong Historical Museum; the New Jersey State Park Service; Bob Parichuk; Al Amey; Mike Kinsella; J. Banks Smither; Sam Baltrusis; Richard Estep; Robert and Sandra Bandov of Bearfort Paranormal; Lisa Parise; Jared Hayter and Evelyn Fuertes; Rachel Weiss; Karen Smyers; the Oakes family; the Kelly family; the Smith and Maynard families; my wife, Kate; the Lenni Lenape, whose homeland this is; and the ghosts of northwestern New Jersey.

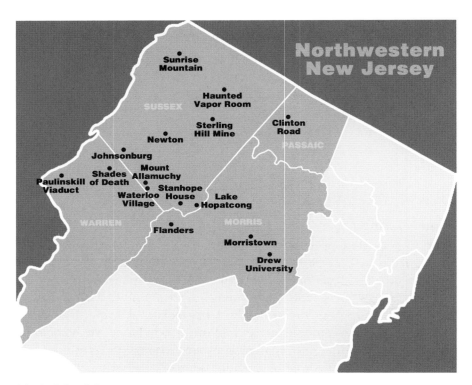

Map by Robert Oakes.

INTRODUCTION

Recently, when I asked a group of my ninth-grade students to write a personal essay, drawing on their earliest memory, I thought it only fair to give myself the same assignment. So I dug in deep and tried to dredge up the very first thing I could remember. A few fragments came, a few faces and places and sounds. But nothing at first was clear. Then suddenly, something strange came out of the fog. I was looking at a row of houses. It must have been on some side street in Nutley, New Jersey, my hometown. And a man went riding by on a horse, passing through the space between two houses. I remember that he had on clothes of another time, some kind of Revolutionary War getup. I heard the clip-clop of horse hooves on the pavement. And then, horse and man vanished behind the next house. And that's it. That's all I remember.

Thinking back on it now, I try to make sense of this strangeness. I mean, what was that? Why do I have this memory? Did I see a ghost? Did I just imagine a man on a horse? Am I remembering a dream? Or could this have actually happened? As unlikely as it may seem that Washington's double would go riding down the streets of suburbia in the mid-1970s, it is possible. In 1976, just a couple years after I was born, many towns across the country were celebrating America's bicentennial with fireworks, speeches and barbecues. For all I know, this might have been some colonial reenactor marching in a patriotic parade.

Or maybe it really was a ghost.

And that's the thing about a memory like this. It's hard to know what to make of it, whether it was real or unreal. It has a feeling of mystery about it. There's a sense that even on ordinary days among the most mundane settings, strange and wonderful things sometimes appear. Like ghosts. And when I look back on my childhood in New Jersey, I remember other mysterious moments like this one, moments when I sensed something strange, felt the presence of the unseen or got that electric spark of a spirit in the air. Yes, even in New Jersey.

Especially in New Jersey.

When I told someone recently that I was working on a book about North Jersey ghosts, she shot back, "There are ghosts in New Jersey?" I tried to understand what made her so incredulous. I guess people think that ghosts can only be found in some ancient castle or in a New England graveyard. I guess they think New Jersey's too busy for ghosts. They forget that spirits can haunt any place where people have lived and died. And many people have lived and died in New Jersey.

"Of course there are ghosts in New Jersey!" I said. I remember hearing stories. I even remember feeling some unusual things in the house I grew up in. In fact, I recently heard that several subsequent owners of the house had to move out because they said it was too haunted. My old house! And let's not forget that it was my home state that gave birth to one of the most wildly successful celebrations of strangeness, *Weird NJ*, which has since expanded well beyond the Garden State.

So yes, I knew I would find plenty of North Jersey ghost stories, but it wasn't until I began working on this book that I came to appreciate just how haunted the place is said to be. Most people know the Jersey Devil, but have you heard of Hoppie the sea serpent of Lake Hopatcong, the phantom Hookerman of Flanders or the spirit of the Sussex Sorcerer? In fact, there are so many ghosts, so many stories and so many reportedly active locations, I had to break this book into two volumes, *Ghosts of Northwestern New Jersey* and *Ghosts of Northeastern New Jersey*.

Of course, when you start to talk about ghosts, the question always comes up: Do they really exist? Some say yes, some say no and others remain uncertain. Honestly, it isn't my intention to answer that question here. To prove or disprove the existence of ghosts is beyond the scope of this book. In the interest of full disclosure, I will say that I do believe that ghosts may exist in our world, and as I said, I have had some unusual experiences of my own, but I know that I don't know. Not really. And I'm comfortable with the mystery. In fact, it's the mystery I love the most. And here's the thing: you don't need to believe in ghosts to love the lore. Similar to what Mark Moran of *Weird NJ* said in a 2014 *New York Daily News* article by Nick Kurczewski, I believe in ghost stories. I believe they are well worth telling. They give us such insight into the people who tell them and the places from which they emerge. They express the mysterious experiences that so many have had but often never talk about publicly. And they are usually intertwined with the roots of a region, often connected to locations that do indeed have a special kind of presence to them. These stories can express that intangible quality and capture a true sense of place. And I also agree with author Edith Wharton, at whose home in the Berkshires I lead ghost tours, who said you don't need to believe in ghosts to be afraid of them, to get the shivers down the spine when you encounter one, whether in the world or in a story.

To me, it is the stories that matter the most, and it's so important to keep them alive. So, for this book, I sought to combine some of northwestern New Jersey's best-known ghost lore with a few tales that seem to have been pretty much forgotten. I tried to include as many firsthand accounts as I could gather, and I'm grateful to those who shared their stories with me. I also tried to provide historical context whenever possible, as accurately as I could. But I'm more of a storyteller than a historian, so I encourage you, if you are interested in the history of New Jersey, to read some of the many wonderful books that have been written by professional historians. I also encourage you to check out the many other online and print publications that celebrate Jersey's ghost lore, several of which served as valuable resources for me. I reference some of them in the chapters that follow, and you'll also find a complete bibliography at the back of this book.

I'd also like to say a word about visiting the places that are featured here. Whenever possible, I like to go to the locations I write about, just to find out what it feels like to be there and to speak with people, if I can. And as a ghost tour guide, I have seen again and again how a walk through a reportedly haunted house can have a powerful effect. So I understand why many may want to go to these places, and as long as it can be done legally, respectfully, responsibly and with permission, I think it can be a meaningful experience. But—and this is something I want to emphasize—I do not condone or encourage illegal or disruptive activity. As we explore this lore, we must never trespass, break the law or cause damage or disturbance.

It's been almost twenty years now since I left New Jersey, and in that time, Western Massachusetts has become my adopted home. But when I saw the chance to write about the ghost lore of my home state, I jumped at it. And just as I hoped it would be, writing this book has been a wonderful homecoming. It has given me a chance to reconnect with old friends while also making new ones, to revisit old haunts while also discovering places I never knew and to rekindle my pride for the state that raised me. I may have moved away almost twenty years ago, but I'll always be from New Jersey.

One of the writers I discovered as I researched Jersey lore was Henry Charlton Beck, an Episcopal minister and folklorist who traveled from town to town, talked to people and wrote down all the lore they could remember. I realized early on in this journey that Beck would become one of my go-to guides. His writings reminded me of the importance of oral history, of the memories of everyday people and of the stories that they tell. These reports may not always make it into the history books, but they are no less significant. They are the voice of the people, their lives and experiences described in their own words. And because Beck put so much stock in these personal histories, he encouraged me to honor my own. So, in that spirit, I decided to include more of myself here than I did in my previous book, *Ghosts of the Berkshires*.

However far away we go, stories take us home. The tales we tell about the people and the places and the moments we remember instantly bring us back to where we're from. This was brought home to me by the inscription I found, written by some unknown hand, in my used copy of Beck's *Roads of Home: The Lanes and Legends of New Jersey*: "Just don't forget where you come from—or us."

"Or our ghosts," I would add.

CHAPTER 1

CALLING QUAQUAHELA FROM THE RIVER STYX BRIDGE

I stood on the bridge over a cove of Lake Hopatcong known as the River Styx, feeling a little shy about what I was about to do. But I had come a long way that day, and now that I was there, I had to try. The traffic roared behind me, and beneath the bridge, a party boat passed. I saw people in tank tops and bikinis drifting by in a cloud of electronic beats and the smell of sunscreen. Someone waved, and I waved back, and then I waited for their eyes to fall away. I stood up tall, took a deep breath and fixed my gaze on the trees across the water.

"Quaquahela!" I called and waited.

"Quaquahela!" I called again.

I guess I felt a little silly. No one else that I could see had come to the lake that day to call for the ghost of a Lenape chief. The woman I had spoken to at the convenience store up the road said she'd never even heard of him, though I did hear her say as she returned to her sweeping, "I like those kinds of stories." But the truth is, I wasn't alone in my search for Quaquahela—at least, that is, if time isn't a separating factor. Because, almost sixty years ago, New Jersey folklorist Henry Charlton Beck did exactly the same thing that I had come to do that day. "I must confide to you," he wrote in 1964, "I have tried the 'friendly whoop' from the bridge that was long ago erected over the Styx, and for some reason I have heard no echo at all." Instead, he recalled, his cry earned him the disgust of a fisherman and the suspicion of a cop. "It is just as well," Beck reflected, "that I did not linger to explain

The view of Lake Hopatcong from the River Styx Bridge. Does the spirit of Quaquahela still watch over the woods and water? *Robert Oakes.*

that I was seeking a return call from Quaquahela." After all, how could they understand if they hadn't even heard the tale?

The story of Quaquahela brings us back to the distant past, to a time before the lake was lined with houses and restaurants, before it was a bucolic nineteenth-century getaway for the wealthy and well connected and even before the earliest Europeans arrived in the 1600s. Long before they came, the Lenape people found here two smaller lakes, known as Great Pond and Little Pond, which had been created when the Wisconsin glacier that once covered much of northern New Jersey receded. For many years, the Nariticong clan of the Lenape lived along the lakeshore in villages and camps, drawing fish from the water and game from the nearby woods. But by the mid-1700s, Europeans had moved in, driving out the Indigenous people and introducing industrial activity that caused profound change to the region. When the mouth of the Musconetcong River was dammed around 1764 to feed the Brookland forge and mill, the water level in Great Pond began to rise, turning some of its jutting promontories into islands. And when an enlarged dam was built in the 1830s to supply water to the Morris Canal, the water rose again, and Great Pond and Little Pond were joined, forming a lake more than six miles long and covering about 2,400 acres, the largest in New Jersey. The lake was called Hopatcong, it is believed, after an ancient Lenape name. The presence of the Lenape can still be felt here in place names like these, as well as in stories like the one about the ghost of Quaquahela.

Long ago, it was said, Quaquahela lived with his people beside the River Styx. One day, he crossed the lake to visit the chief of a neighboring tribe. But on the far shore, he was brutally attacked by a bear, and though the sachem was armed with a war club and knife, he refused to fight. The bear was his totem, and to kill it was forbidden. So he tried to run, but the bear was too quick, leaving Quaquahela no choice. Knife and claw clashed, and blood soaked the muddy banks as man and beast battled on the lakeshore. Quaquahela killed his attacker but suffered a fatal wound. In the morning, the men of the neighboring tribe found the bear and the sachem's bloody club, but there was no trace of his body; instead, they found only paw prints in the mud and concluded it had been dragged off by a pack of wolves, never to be recovered.

On the night of the next full moon, the Nariticong, still mourning the loss of their beloved chief, were amazed to see a thin form of mist curl above the trees on the hillside near the lake, like the smoke of a campfire. And though the wind was strong that night, the curl of mist remained unmoved. The medicine man of the clan sensed meaning in this occurrence and fell asleep that night with anticipation. In his dream, he was visited by the spirit of Quaquahela, who said it was he they had seen as a mist and that because he had killed the sacred bear, his ghost must wander the world, forever in exile from spirit-land. And there, where they had seen the mist rise, Quaquahela built his spirit lodge. There he would remain. So long as the hills were standing, Quaquahela would keep watch over his people and the lake on which they lived. He vowed to guard them and to guide them. And if they ever wanted to know that he was there, they needed only to look for the mist on the hillside. And if they ever wanted his guidance, they needed only to call. It is said that the mist can still be seen above the lake and trees on damp days. And anyone who calls for Quaquahela near the River Styx will hear his spirit echo in reply.

It's unclear to me whether this tale was ever told by the Nariticong themselves. It seems more likely that it was made up by those who wished to sell the region as a tourist destination in the nineteenth century, though it is possible it was based upon existing lore. The earliest written records of the story that I could find were published in the late 1800s. The first is in *The History of Morris County, New Jersey* by Edmund Halsey, published in 1882. The second is in a book called *The Central Railroad of New Jersey, An Illustrated Guide-Book* by Gustav Kobbé, published in 1890 to promote travel along the Jersey Central railway line. Kobbé described the region's bucolic beauty at the end of the nineteenth century with all the romanticism he could muster:

When the lake lies like a mirror in the moonlight there is heard a murmuring among the hills, like a low, melodious chanting of many distant voices; and one half fancies that the nymphs and naiads have come forth from the shaded springs and rills of the forest and gathered upon some moonlit meadow far up on the mountain to celebrate the glories of the night.

Kobbé also suggested a darker, more mysterious presence in the lake, especially near the River Styx, which may have given rise to tales of ghosts. The shadows cast on the black water, decaying trees and jagged branches, the gloomy recesses of the forest and a strange stillness "combine to so impress the traveler on the Styx with a sense of the mysterious and supernatural that he is ready to accept, without questioning, the legend of the…spirit…said to haunt the depths of the forest back of the south arm of the inlet."

Over the years, many have commented on the mists that sometimes settle over Lake Hopatcong and seem to sense something otherworldly in them. As recent social media posts attest, such curiosity about the mists continues to this day. And back in 1964, Beck wrote about a conversation that he had with an old steamboat skipper named Bill Gordon who could remember

Some have sensed a dark, mysterious presence in the lake, especially near the River Styx, which may have given rise to tales of ghosts. *Katherine Oakes.*

"days…when the mists off the lake were slowly climbing up the mountains." This recollection led Beck to wonder, "Could not the mists sometimes be the smoke of a lonely Indian's fire? Could it not be that…Quaquahela, unknown to the modern generation of rush and rattle, [is] still up there, somewhere between the River Styx and Lubber's Run?"

Maybe, though it does seem more likely that the spirit of Quaquahela would have moved on with the Nariticong. But if he is still watching over the lake, would those who live there today recognize him, as Kobbé wrote, in a "mist ascending to the heavens?" If we called out to him, would we receive an answer? Could he even hear us over the party boats and cars? I guess that's what I had come that day to learn.

Just like Beck, I heard no echo when I called to Quaquahela. Nevertheless, as I've delved into the ghost lore of my home state, traveling to different places and speaking with those who have stories to tell, I have often felt the presence of a guiding spirit leading me on to the next destination or discovery. And since Quaquahela was said to guide those who call to him, I had to wonder whether I had made contact after all.

Beck believed in these old stories. He praised how they persist "no matter how much an era of speed…and gadgets ignores them." Surely, the story of Quaquahela, and the spirit it contains, must live on in our memory for some reason. And maybe, if we listen, and if we send our call, we'll get the guidance we forgot we needed.

CHAPTER 2

MORE GHOSTS AND BEASTS OF LAKE HOPATCONG

Quaquahela isn't the only spirit said to have emerged from the shadows of Lake Hopatcong. In his 1956 book *The Roads of Home: Lanes and Legends of New Jersey*, Beck made a passing reference to a ghost that sang on dark winter nights somewhere near the lake. And there have also been recent reports of spirits lingering in some of the homes that hug the shoreline. But tales of ghosts haunting these lakeside houses are nothing new. An article published in the *New York World* newspaper on January 15, 1894, told of the ghost of the Minton place, an "empty, forlorn old house" near the Woodport area of the lake about which "queer stories have been whispered…for many years." According to the article, a local man named Sol Babcock, who had come to investigate the "strange doings" in the house, at first considered it all a "passel o' nonsense," but after staying the night there, Sol had a change of heart. He said he heard footsteps going up and down the stairs at one o'clock in the morning when everybody else in the house was asleep. He also claimed to hear tubs moving around in the cellar, chairs moving in a room on the first floor and loaves of bread being slung against the pantry door. But what scared Sol Babcock the most was what came through the cellar door. Said Sol:

> *The latch…raises of itself and the door opens of itself and a cold gust of air comes rushing into the room like it came out of a graveyard vault….* [Then] *a waxy white hand without any arm or any lodging for human*

vitals comes up out of the cellar, carrying a sort of blue light, and then goes poking around the room at just about the height a person would carry it, and then goes upstairs and holds itself over sleeping people's faces, like it wanted to make sure they were not the ones it was looking for.

Charles Babcock, who had lived in the house before being driven out by the paranormal activity, said he considered the cellar to be "the center of disturbance." He claimed that his wife's griddle was repeatedly taken down the cellar stairs or propped up against the inside of the cellar door. Charles also said he often heard footsteps slowly ascending the stairs leading to his bedroom, where they would stop. But his most startling claim involved a lamp in the bedroom, which he had left on very low one night. "I had been asleep some time when I was suddenly awakened by the room being brilliantly lighted. I sprang up in bed. The lamp was turned up to its fullest extent." When he jumped from bed to lower the lamp, he said, it suddenly dimmed again, but "as it went down, I saw or imagined I saw a shadowy, misty sort of figure in general outline like that of a human being standing by the table." As the figure "seemed to melt away," Charles said, he heard footsteps descend the stairs toward the cellar door.

According to the article, the Minton house "looked dismal and forlorn enough to be the scene of almost any form of diablerie that might be imagined," so much so that people began "to give it a wide berth at night as they [went] over the lonely mountain roads to and from their homes."

Others, though, were drawn to it. Pioneering investigative journalist Nellie Bly, whose exploits were recounted in an article published in the February 4, 1894 edition of the *New York World*, stayed alone one night at the Minton house, "armed with two pistols," in order to debunk the claims. "Oh, I was brave, dreadfully brave," wrote Bly, "but that was before I spent a night alone in the haunted Minton house in New Jersey."

According to Bly, the ghost that haunted the house was said to be "the spirit of a young and beautiful girl [who] was murdered there and buried in the cellar…[and later] was seen in the barn milking a spook cow with one horn."

But in the face of such reports and all the local gossip, Bly remained skeptical, though she was not without fear. "I was not afraid of ghosts, at least I thought so. I did not believe in them…but I did fear my imagination, my nerves. I feared myself." Bly said she also feared meeting "tramps, or counterfeiters, or moonshiners…[or] half a dozen burly men with shaggy beards and rough clothes" in that "desolate, wild place."

What's most striking about Bly's article is the way she describes this "lonely, God-forsaken region." How remote and isolated "the bleak hills of New Jersey" must have seemed then, especially to a journalist from New York City. She wrote:

> *I was to go…out into a wild, unsettled part of the country to a vacant house that has been much written about as haunted. This house—very old and dilapidated—stands alone, surrounded by hills and wild woods. The nearest habitation is a mile distant across fields that none but a spirit could cross, and heaven knows how far it is off by road.…Lonely did not begin to describe the country through which we were passing.*

And though she was brave, the deeper Bly passed into the wilderness, the more frightened she became. "The rough road we traveled was straight through heavy woods…[and] every dark shadow or bush I saw made my flesh creep."

Bly did experience strange noises in the house that night, as well as doors that seemed to open on their own, but she was able to explain it all away: icy snow tapping on the windows, wind blowing through the chimney, the moaning and creaking of an old house settling. And the opening doors? Well, that was only her little dog, Paddy. "I had given all things supernatural all the chance in the world to make a decent and startling appearance," she wrote. "I was ready and willing…to behold their ghastly forms and to report their tales of woe in all truthfulness, if it was their pleasure to speak. But… the ghosts did not come; neither did tramps, I am glad to say."

Nellie Bly may have found no ghosts in the Minton house, but that made it no less of an attraction. An article in the July 10, 1909 edition of the *Lake Hopatcong Breeze* refers to the "annual pilgrimages" made by many summer visitors to "the Haunted House," which, according to the article "stood near the sawmill on Prospect Point." Fully abandoned to the ghosts, the house was finally lost to fire in the spring of 1909.

Some of the supernatural entities said to haunt Lake Hopatcong are not ghosts at all. While most people know the most famous of all New Jersey cryptids, the Jersey Devil, some may be surprised to learn that Lake Hopatcong boasts one of its own, a giant serpentine creature known as Hoppie. Said to be as thick as a man's leg with a head the size of a St. Bernard and the body of a forty-foot snake, Hoppie has stirred the waters since his appearance was first reported in the *Lake Hopatcong Angler* on August 4, 1894. Many at the time claimed to see the creature swimming near the

Summer visitors made pilgrimages to the haunted Minton House until it was lost to fire in the spring of 1909. *Lake Hopatcong Historical Museum.*

River Styx. One man said he shot at it, but his bullet "rolled off like water off a duck's back without even making the monster wink." Some at the time dismissed the sea serpent panic, blaming it all on an old mud turtle with a head "like a lager beer keg." And the *Angler* reporter seemed at a loss "to determine whether it was a dog, turtle or beer keg." Nevertheless, the legend of Hoppie has persisted down through the years. And in 2014, when local residents claimed to see a boa constrictor or anaconda snake swimming in the lake, some drew parallels to the sighting of 1894 and wondered whether Hoppie had returned.

In *Weird NJ*, authors Mark Sceurman and Mark Moran mention an even older and more frightening legend of a beast in the lake with a horselike head, a rack of antlers and a body so large it would dwarf an ox. According to the story, the Lenape believed the beast died after falling through the ice in winter and that its bones could be seen beneath the surface.

CHAPTER 3

THE CAMPFIRE GHOSTS OF MOUNT ALLAMUCHY

FRENCHE'S HAUNTED CASTLE

On a rainy August evening, I found myself trekking the woods around Mount Allamuchy Scout Reservation in Byram Township, breathlessly keeping pace with Carl Zipper. I had come there to learn what more there was to the story of James Frenche's haunted castle, about which I had found only tantalizing tidbits in Beck's *Tales and Towns*, some old newspapers and the odd post on social media.

In the late 1940s, Henry Charlton Beck embarked on a similar expedition. Searching for the story of nineteenth-century industrialist James Frenche and his old stone mansion, known as the Castle because of its tower, Beck also went trudging through the Allamuchy grounds. His depictions evoked adventure. He called the mountain "a land of mystery" and said that the "traveler is truly intrepid who pushes through across the mountain from either end." And as he tried to get at the story, Beck also spoke with the Scouts, as well as some trappers, residents and a bartender or two—anyone who could tell him more about Frenche, his mansion and his many industrial activities and experiments up there on the mountain. Oddly, it seemed that, in spite of all this activity, few locals at the time could remember Frenche or his work. Though they may have heard about the ghosts in the ruined castle, no one could recall why, or by whom, it had been built.

Finding the structure at last, Beck described it this way: "With all the dignity of a ruined monastery, the towered 'castle' pointed its roofless 'belfry'

James Frenche's stone mansion, known as the Castle because of its tower, inspired many ghostly tales. *Carl Zipper's collection.*

like a torn finger into the sky." He also came upon "an even more impressive structure, built of fitted stone....[and] the walls of a stone house...probably the oldest structure of all."

What Beck had found was not only the ruins of the castle but also the remnants of a deserted industrial village known as Stourport, what he called "the little kingdom of stone [Frenche] had built and evidently had run with feudal glory." But apart from a few casual mentions, he seemed to have uncovered very little about the ghosts.

In my own search for the ghosts of Frenche's castle, I had been told that Scout volunteer Carl Zipper was the man to see, and about all things Mount Allamuchy and Frenche, he did not disappoint. That evening, he shared with me a wealth of local history and told me about the property's many lives, from the Lenape village, to the Revolutionary-era charcoal kilns, to the nineteenth-century industrial settlement, up to the present-day Scout reservation. Carl's knowledge was encyclopedic, but his approach was anything but bookish. After only a few words of welcome, we were off on our own adventure, trudging through undergrowth and thorns, sliding over slippery river stones and threading the granite outcrops. He showed me the ruins of a factory, warehouse and sawmill; the burned-out land where one of the colonial kilns once lay; flooded and collapsed mineshafts; and the few bricks and shards that are all that now remain of Frenche's castle, the unstable ruins that Beck had explored having been torn down

Carl showed me the ruins of a sawmill and other remnants of the industrial village that once stood on the Allamuchy grounds. *Robert Oakes.*

There are still signs of Frenche's presence on the grounds of Mount Allamuchy Scout Reservation. *Robert Oakes.*

by the Scouts decades ago, then paved over some years later during the construction of the interstate. But Beck's book, old photographs and old-timers' recollections all testify to the crumbling stonework that once stood on that spot, the same crumbling stones among the creepers and trees that appear to have inspired the tales. Some old Scouts fondly remember the first time they heard those stories, as recent social media posts attest. They recall the ruins of the old castle, the creepy tales and the sound of howls in the haunted woods that kept them up all night.

Despite all our trudging and trekking, the ghosts of Frenche's castle remained elusive. Like the castle itself, only fragments of the stories endure. Remembrances like those online posts point to their existence, but the details are all but forgotten. Still, I was happy to discover that day that not all of the ghosts of Mount Allamuchy have been lost. Some live on in new stories told by Scouters like Carl, which he was obliging enough to share with me.

Mercifully, Carl waited until we were back in the dry safety of the camp before sharing this eerie tale of an unsolved disappearance, mysterious blue lights and an ancient evil that is said to haunt the mountain. What follows is that story, in Carl's own words, just as he tells it by campfire light to the Scouts of Allamuchy.

THE ANCIENT EVIL OF MOUNT ALLAMUCHY, AS TOLD BY CARL ZIPPER

This camp has a very long history going all the way back to the Lenape people. There was an Indian village near the present site of the camp office, and legend has it that, up in the woods, somewhere at the north end of the property, there was once a Lenape ceremonial site called the Wolf's Den, though no one knows what it looked like or what exactly it was for. Colonial surveyor John Reading Jr., one of the first colonists to walk this land when he surveyed it in 1715, wrote in his journal that, though the Lenape were afraid of the Wolf's Den, they would go there to perform ceremonies meant to appease some great evil. And Reading further wrote that the Lenape wouldn't let him go there, but they had surrounded the area where he believed the Wolf's Den to be with totem poles. It was his understanding that the totem poles were treated with medicine to keep whatever was in the Wolf's Den at bay.

Now, by 1715, the time of the Lenape was coming to a close, and they soon were forced under some degree of duress and some degree of economic pressure to sell out to the proprietors of the West Jersey Society. This particular piece of land was surveyed to William Penn, the founder of Pennsylvania and one of the West Jersey proprietors, who sold it on to other speculators. Eventually, the land was purchased by two wealthy Philadelphia merchants named Turner and Allen, who developed an iron forge near here and logged and burned this property for charcoal to heat the iron ore. In the process, the totem poles were cut down, and the Lenape medicine went with them. And whatever it was the Lenape were trying to keep at bay was no longer held back.

The turmoil of the Revolution caused the forge to fail, and the land went back to forest. Decades passed before it was purchased by an Englishman named John Humphries, who cut down what trees had grown back and built two lakes and a factory, where he made carpets. And just like the iron forge before it, the carpet factory also didn't work out. Humphries lost his fortune, died and was buried in an unmarked grave in the churchyard at Waterloo.

Before he died, Humphries sold the property to an ambitious Irish immigrant named James Frenche. Frenche repurposed the factory for flax to make linen thread and twine, but he had grander ambitions. He wanted to be more than a flaxman. He wanted to be a true robber baron in the grand nineteenth-century tradition. He believed there was potential in this property, in the trees and in the stones. Maybe he could develop an iron mine, or maybe he could sell the trees for lumber.

And so he brought in two experts to give him their opinion. The first was a forester who knew trees, and the second was a geologist, an expert in prospecting for iron. These two men came in on horseback, hiked up to the high ground near the north end of the property and set up their camp, a canvas tent with cots inside, much like we still camp in today. There they got ready for a hard week's work, tramping over the land: the geologist with his dip needle and compass, searching for iron ore, and the forester with his axe, sounding the trees and cutting blazes—both men trying to find a fortune for Frenche.

On the first day, they went out and surveyed for iron and timber. At night, they returned to their campsite and sat down to write about the day's findings in their journal, enjoying the beautiful sights from the top of the hill. As the sun went down, they noticed, way off in the distance, miles and miles away, something very unusual. They saw spots of blue light like nothing they'd ever seen before. And they thought, *That's strange. We've been to many places, and we've seen many things, but we've never seen anything like that.* So they wrote it down in their journal and turned in for the night.

The next morning, they set off again to hammer rocks, bang on trees and take notes. And after another hard day's work, they met back up at the campsite and cooked up their dinner on the fire. And as they were writing their notes, they looked out, and what did they see? Just like the night before, they saw the same blue lights, only this time they were a little bit closer, only about a mile away. And they thought, *Perhaps those blue lights are some sort of unknown atmospheric phenomenon.* So, again, they wrote it down in their journal and turned in for the night.

And for the next two days, the geologist searched for iron while the forester surveyed the trees, each man writing down his findings in the journal. And each of the next two nights, as they collected their notes from the day's work, the blue lights would appear, each time a little bit closer. They could see the lights; they could see that they were getting nearer, but they couldn't see exactly what they were. All they could see were hazy points of light. So they wrote it down in the journal, though they had no idea what it was they were witnessing. And they thought, *Oh, good Lord. This is just about the strangest thing*

For the next two nights, the blue lights would appear, each night a little bit closer. *Katherine Oakes.*

we've ever seen. And we're learned men. We're men of science. And yet we don't know anything about this. What we need is a meteorologist.

Now, the problem was, in those days, if you wanted to find a meteorologist, you had to go to the city, in this case New York City. But here they were, way out in the wilderness of New Jersey. Now, they knew Frenche would have their hides if they both left the job to go find a meteorologist, so the forester, who had largely finished his survey, offered to ride to Dover and take the train to New York while the geologist stayed behind to investigate the one location he had yet to explore fully: the north end of the property.

So the next day they woke up early, and the forester said his goodbyes, promising to return in two days with the meteorologist. The geologist was excited to explore the north end because, the day before, he had started to get some strong response in that direction with his dip needle. *It was really jumping around*, he thought. *I think I might be on to something.* So he packed up his compass and his notebook, and he headed toward the north end of the property to see what he might find.

In two days' time, the forester returned with a meteorologist just as the sun was starting to set. And as they huffed and puffed their way up the hill to the campsite, the forester pictured the nice hot pot of stew he knew the geologist would have going on the fire. He thought, *We'll get up there, we'll eat and then maybe we'll be able to see those blue lights tonight.*

But as they reached the top of the hill, they found nobody there. They weren't worried, because they saw that the flaps of the geologist's tent were tied shut from the inside, so they knew that he must be in there. They figured, *Well, he must have been working hard today. He's probably taking a rest, so we won't disturb him.* So they chopped wood, they got the fire going and they got the stew on, but even through all that noise, the geologist still didn't stir.

"I thought for sure he'd be up by now," the forester said. "I guess we're going to have to wake him." So they started knocking on the tent and calling for him, but they got no response.

Now they started getting worried, thinking that the man had overexerted himself and collapsed in his tent of a heart attack. *He's probably dead in there on his cot*, they thought. So they cut the ties on the tent and went in, only to find no one there. The cots were there. The bedding was made up nicely. But there was no geologist. On the little table beside his cot, they saw a candle burned all the way down to nothing, leaving just a pool of wax. And they also saw the man's journal lying there, left open.

"Something must have come up," the forester said. "He probably left us a note in there to explain what's going on."

So he picked up the journal and began to read it. He found the record of the day's exploration. And just in the middle of something about a mine that the geologist had found, all of a sudden, the writing trailed off, a couple of lines were skipped, and then he started writing something new. Now, I can quote it to you exactly, because I've seen the journal myself. What he wrote was this: "It is nighttime again and the blue lights are back. They are all around the tent just outside. They say that I must go with them. I am going." And that was all he wrote.

Although it was dark, they went out to look for the geologist. They looked all over, but they couldn't find him anywhere, not that night and not the next day either. They got on their horses and searched all over, clanging pots and pans, shooting guns in the air, yelling and hollering. But they never found a trace of him. They never found the blue lights either. The meteorologist stayed up each night looking, but like the geologist, there wasn't even the faintest trace. And to this day, no one knows what happened to the man. His body has never been found, not even a skull or bone. Nothing. People still talk about the blue lights and the missing geologist. People still wonder.

Some say he probably fell down a deep crevasse where his body could not be found. Others say that he was deep in debt and that he faked his death to make a new start. Now, the best speculation that I've heard is that the geologist was on to something, all right, but it wasn't a mine. He found something much, much worse. And whatever it was that he found, it found him too. Maybe it was something in the Wolf's Den, the evil that the Lenape had long kept at bay, maybe it was something else, but I'll tell you this: where we are right now is about as far north as I like to go in this camp.

CARL WAS CAREFUL TO point out that while the broad historical outline of his story is true, its supernatural particulars are not. As I see it, it perfectly demonstrates how legends are born out of history. And it confirmed what I already suspected: if you want to hear a good ghostly yarn, go see the Scouts. After all, scaring young Scouts by the light of a campfire is as much a Scouting tradition as neckerchiefs and merit badges. And to watch Carl embody this deep-rooted storytelling tradition warmed my heart as it chilled my spine.

Carl's was not the only ghost story I was told at Allamuchy. During my visit, I was also introduced to another piece of well-known Sussex County Scout lore and to the man who could tell it to me, head commissioner

George Pantos, who has been leading Scouts—and telling tales—for more than twenty-five years. It is the story of the Purple Bishop, a troubled soul who walks the woods at night seeking justice and vengeance against those who betrayed him. And according to George, it has long been one of the mainstays of campfire lore in Scouting.

"It goes way back," he said. "I don't know exactly what the roots of the story are, but I'm sure it goes back even before the 1950s when I first heard it."

It was the summer of 1959, and eleven-year-old George was at sleepaway camp for the very first time.

> *It was scary, even though my older brother was with me and the other fellas from my troop. But you're away. You're out in the woods. You're living the life of a Scout out there, miles away from home. And you're not going home at night. This isn't day camp anymore.*

So, naturally, Scoutmasters thought a good ghost story would help ease their minds. George recalled, "This story scared the living heck out of me and out of every other young fellow that heard it off in the woods." Still, he wasn't too scared to tell it to me, just as he heard it that night. What follows is the story, as told by George.

THE PURPLE BISHOP, AS TOLD BY GEORGE PANTOS

Ah, the Purple Bishop. That's a sad, strange story, for sure, especially when you think about how close we are to where much of it happened.

I heard his name was Reverend O'Malley and that he came from a big-city church somewhere east of here. The story goes that the Reverend was special, gifted and devout and had a large congregation that respected him greatly and followed his teachings. But above all his wonderful preaching, he cherished the beautiful, hand-carved wooden crucifix that hung over the altar. It was as if he and the cross were one, the physical part of his eternal soul.

But one night, some young boys from the neighborhood decided to prank him by vandalizing the church. They snuck in and started turning over pews, throwing hymnals and Bibles around and breaking things. The Reverend heard them and rushed out of his apartment to stop the destruction, begging them to stop. The boys panicked and ran, and as they fled, they knocked over several lit candles. The torn-up hymnals and Bibles caught fire, and it quickly spread to the carpet and pews. The Reverend saw that the fire was growing out of control and realized it would quickly consume the entire church. So, through the growing flames, he ran to the altar to save the cross, and shielding it with his body, he climbed over the flaming pews and burst out of the church's double doors, where he collapsed on its steps, clutching the cross to his chest.

When rescuers arrived, they found Reverend O'Malley on the steps, vestments and clothing smoldering, blackened and burned away. Worse, they saw the damage the flames had done to him—his face horribly burned, hair, ears and nose almost gone, hands and arms stripped of skin, legs singed raw and blistering. But the beautiful cross was untouched due to his incredible personal sacrifice to save it. Even in his incredible pain, he was still grasping it in his ruined hands.

As he slowly recovered, he knew he could never go back to the parish he once loved so dearly. His face and body were horribly scarred, and he did not want to be seen by his parishioners looking like a monster. But the fire devastated more than his body—it burned his mind and soul as well, filling him with doubt about the goodness of man and God. The memory of the boys laughing, the flames wildly burning him and the searing pain turned his love of mankind into resentment, scorn and disgust. His bitterness grew with each passing day. Only his beloved cross, which he kept ever close to him, gave him strength and comforted his soul.

He found a position as pastor of a small private chapel here in northwest New Jersey. At first, people came to hear him speak, but they quickly became disillusioned with his words. Where once he spoke of God's love, he now preached God's wrath, berating people for their impure thoughts and actions, focusing on sin and punishment and warning people of the terrible judgment awaiting them.

Even more upsetting to the dwindling number of parishioners were his vestments and appearance. He wore purple robes—bishop's vestments—with a hood to mask his destroyed face and purple gloves to conceal his ruined hands. He lit the chapel with purple-colored candles and lanterns. Purple—the color of the fire that consumed him years before. Purple—the color of his sadness and anger. Purple—the color of our campfire.

Reverend O'Malley knew his end was approaching, and believing the chapel would likely be abandoned after his death, he asked to be buried in full purple vestments under the wide second step in front of the chapel, along with his beloved crucifix, and that a small purple light be eternally fixed above his grave to give his troubled spirit comfort and peace. He made it clear that he would hold those responsible to this promise, even from his grave.

When his time came, Reverend O'Malley was laid to rest under the church step as he wished, purple light and all, but with one exception. It was decided that the crucifix should remain hanging in the chapel above the altar, as it had significant monetary value. In time, it became a legend and a curiosity among the local people. For years, it drew visitors who wanted to see the Purple Bishop's cross.

But for Reverend O'Malley, who lay in that shallow grave under the church steps without his cross, it was a sacred oath shattered and an act of irredeemable sin. His flame-darkened spirit was not at peace in the afterlife.

Years passed, and as Reverend O'Malley predicted, the chapel was abandoned. Though it remained standing and the cross continued to hang over the altar, no tourists came to see the old church anymore. No one cared for the building. Its road became overgrown, weeds and vines grew all around it and it fell into decay. It became a dark, broken shell deep in the woods, virtually forgotten by everyone.

That is, until decades later, when three boys on a camping trip came across the fallen-down chapel in the woods while looking for firewood—it was boarded up, overgrown and abandoned. Back at camp, they decided they would break into it to see if anything of value was there. Since it was clearly deserted, they thought no one would care.

Later that night, they came with flashlights, a sledgehammer and other tools to force their way in. Once inside, in the pitch darkness, with only flashlights to guide them, they started turning over pews and breaking into cabinets and wall panels, searching for valuables, laughing as they swung the heavy sledgehammer into the walls and marble altar. The stone slab shattered under the heavy blows, and the boys laughed, tracing its fragments with their lights as they flew into the coal-black air.

That's when they saw it, caught in the beams of the flashlights, hanging exactly where Reverend O'Malley had placed it over the now-shattered altar: the crucifix of the Purple Bishop. It seemed to glow and pulse with an internal energy—as if it were alive. *This must have some real value*, they thought. *Let's take it and cash in on it*, they thought, as they pulled the cross from its sacred place above the ruined altar.

That's when they heard it: a muffled rustling sound coming from the front of the church, a faint scraping, as though something was moving uneasily

The hooded figure slowly emerged from its grave, a grotesque figure dressed in decaying purple robes, its gnarled, claw-like hand holding a purple lantern. *Katherine Oakes.*

under the decaying chapel steps. It was a low sound, vaguely familiar but still alien, like softly crinkling paper or a cat scratching at the door to be let in, hardly noticeable but definitely there. They shined their flashlights toward the sound, but nothing was there, only that sound they could now hear clearly within the midnight darkness. It was getting louder and more intense. And closer.

Fearing that someone was coming to find them looting and vandalizing the place, the boys scrambled to get out, carelessly grabbing their tools, lights and, of course, the crucifix. It was a jumble in the dark, the three of them bumping into each other and the pews, tripping over rotten floorboards, dropping their flashlights as they ran wildly toward the door. They stumbled out into the dark night, but in their haste and fear, one of them dropped the heavy sledgehammer onto the chapel's step—the chapel's second step, the Purple Bishop's grave.

The heavy hammer cracked the slab in two, and as they looked back, they saw a dim purple glow coming from the broken step. Terrified, they froze, staring as the crack grew wider, stone scraping on stone, making a skin-crawling sound like fingernails on a chalkboard. The dim purple light grew stronger. Petrified by fear, they stood and watched as a hooded figure slowly emerged from the steps—its grave—a grotesque, unearthly figure dressed in decaying purple robes, its gnarled, claw-like hand holding a purple lantern.

Now beyond fear, they ran for their lives, throwing away anything that would slow them down as they stumbled and crashed through the weeds, roots and vines clutching at their legs. Everything, that is, except the crucifix, the beloved cross of the Purple Bishop.

For days, search parties scoured the forest around the boys' campsite but found nothing except their empty tents and camping gear. In the ruins of the chapel, they found some tools, two flashlights with dead batteries and a baseball cap belonging to one of the boys. They also found a heavy sledgehammer by the chapel's cracked front step and an old, almost illegible grave marker, dislodged from its base, lying on the broken steps. The grave it had marked was empty.

Newspapers reported that the search would continue until the boys were found, but after a few weeks, it was called off. The boys were never heard from again, and the chapel's ruins were torn down, leaving only the broken remains of its stone foundation.

That's pretty much all there is to tell.

But there is one more thing. Over the years, there have been reports by campers around here of a strange purple light glowing far off, deep in the forest. It appears late at night, usually after midnight and after their campfires have been burning brightly for a while. Some witnesses report the light moving slowly to the left or right, as if something out there were circling them. Others state that the light remains in one spot for hours, as if someone were watching them, waiting. All agree that it eventually disappears, particularly as dawn approaches.

Could it be the Purple Bishop looking for his lost and stolen cross? Could he be searching for it among campers, like those who desecrated his resting place and stole the remains of his earthly essence so long ago? Could it be his tortured spirit, longing for peace that can only be found when it is reunited with his beloved cross? Or is it his angry soul seeking revenge for the loss of faith, betrayal and horrible disfigurement he suffered?

I don't know—I guess no one ever will. But on nights like this, even after all the campfires I've sat around have burned down to flickering embers, light and heat no longer radiating protection from unknown things and shadows in the night, I still find myself staring into the forest, looking for a dim purple glow in the darkness.

THAT VERY FIRST TELLING of "The Purple Bishop" back in the summer of 1959 burned itself deep into George's memory.

"I remember it as if it were yesterday," he said. "I've never forgotten the story, and of course I've retold it many times. Put me in front of a campfire and ask me to tell a story, and this is one I'm likely to tell—with the appropriate embellishments to suit the situation, if you know what I mean."

"Embellishments?" I asked.

"You know, you have someone dress as the Purple Bishop and come out of the woods, or you have someone with a purple light moving through the darkness outside the perimeter of the campfire, or you have someone in the woods making cracking noises, stepping on branches and all that. You gotta give it a little bit of showbiz."

And whenever he tells the tale at Allamuchy, George also makes effective use of the old stone ruins of Frenche's industrial village.

"You can say, 'Do you see that foundation? Do you see those rocks there? Guess what that was. That was the Purple Bishop's chapel, the one that burned down. They tried to cover it up, but you never know.' And here you are huddling around a crackling campfire under the stars, and it's bright as can be for the perimeter of your light. But beyond the perimeter, it's pitch black. You can't see anything. And you say, 'You never know what's out there in the pitch-black woods. Who knows who could be watching us?' You read the crowd, and you see how they're reacting, and you throw things in to make it more effective."

"And how do the kids react?"

"They say, 'Oh my God! Oh my God! Oh my God!' Especially if someone is out there cracking a stick or walking around with a flashlight with a purple gel on it. 'Oh my God! What's that light? Oh my God!' But they love it. They say, 'Tell us another one!' They want to hear it. They want a good scare."

One of the reasons why George believes the story works so well is because it captures the fear of the unknown in an unfamiliar place. "'What's that noise? Who's that behind me? I can't see what's over there?' When you're a young kid and you're in an alien environment, you're by yourself, you're sitting out there around this fire. And the fire is this warm, comforting thing. But it's also a beacon. And there's someone out there looking to find where the people are. You want to stay close to the fire, but of course, the fire is the thing that's bringing him in."

George also believes the story to be timeless because the spirit is driven by something everyone can relate to. "He was horribly wronged, and he will never be at peace until he is given his justice, that is, getting his cross back. So there's a sense of the restlessness of a spirit in search of something important. He's a religious man looking for justice and peace. He recognizes there is evil in the world. He's been victimized by it, and he's on a quest to try to assuage his pain by reconnecting with this crucifix that he loved."

It's especially effective that "he's not a murderer and he's not a monster. Believe it or not, it's scarier to the kids for it not to be a monster. Psychological fear is much more terrifying. They wonder, 'What is he going to do if he finds us? What's going to happen?' That's why we don't have him killing and eating people, only that he's out there and he's searching. And you say, 'So when you see that light, you know it's the Purple Bishop,' and you leave it at that. 'When the tent flap flutters at night, or when you hear a scratching sound, it could be just a breeze or a moth, or it could be the Purple Bishop.'"

CHAPTER 4

GHOST TOWN

WATERLOO VILLAGE

I t was late in the day as I pulled into the parking lot at historic Waterloo Village in Byram Township. Some heavy weather was in the forecast, and the clouds looked like they were about to burst. But I figured I had time for a quick walk through the village before the skies opened up, enough time to look around and get a feel for the place again. After all, it had been about twenty-five years since I was last there, and things seemed a little different.

For starters, no one was around—no one I could see, anyway. Last time, there were docents and artisans, families and school groups. This time, it was only me, a cautious woodchuck and some unusually docile deer.

And ghosts? Well, apart from a porch light that seemed to turn itself on and off, I experienced nothing unusual, no apparitions or disembodied voices. But as I peered through the windows of the empty buildings and looked into the mist along the wooded paths, I certainly felt the presence of the unseen, the faded memory of the many lives lived on this land.

For hundreds of years, the Lenape people lived here in villages of their own. But in the mid-1700s, Europeans began to settle along the nearby Musconetcong River, pushing the Lenape out. Soon after, when iron was discovered in the surrounding hills, the Andover Forge was established on this site for the production of wrought iron. The forge remained active through the American Revolution until falling into decline during the early years of the nineteenth century. When the Morris Canal was built in the 1830s, the languishing settlement suddenly found itself at the center of the action, perfectly situated at the midpoint of this highly trafficked commercial waterway that connected the Delaware River to the New York Harbor. Waterloo was reborn and grew quickly into a booming canal town spearheaded by the Smith family, who then owned much of the land. The addition of a nearby railway line in the 1850s only increased the town's prosperity. But the twentieth century brought changes to the railways and waterways, and it wasn't long before the town again went into decline, finally being abandoned to hobos who would jump from passing boxcars and stay overnight on the grounds. In the mid-1900s, after decades of decay, Percival Leach and his partner Louis Gualandi took up ownership of the property, overseeing its restoration and opening it to the public as a living history museum and cultural venue. Today, Waterloo Village is owned by the State of New Jersey and operated as a state park and historic site, featuring a general store, a hotel and tavern, a blacksmith shop, a gristmill and a sawmill, as well as Victorian-style homes, tenant houses and a church. Though the village suffered some setbacks and closures over the past fifteen years, a $3 million state grant, awarded in 2019, promises once again to breathe new life into this historic site.

From what I could gather, there has been a fair amount of recent interest in paranormal activity at the village, enough to inspire museum staff to create the Shadows of the Past, a lantern-lit tour that blends history with legend and accounts of mysterious experiences. The site has also been visited by a number of local paranormal investigation groups, such as the New Jersey Paranormal Project and the Lady Ghostbusters, who have explored the site and documented their findings in videos posted online.

And, of course, there are the stories. One of the oldest tells of the ghost of a boatman who killed himself after his wife left him for another man. Henry Charlton Beck mentioned it in 1956 in *The Roads of Home*, and it appeared again in 2013 in *The Big Book of New Jersey Ghost Stories* by Martinelli and Stansfield, who shed a little more light on the spirit's personality and circumstances. The authors describe the ghost as that of a guilt-stricken man walking slowly beside the canal at Waterloo. This ghost, whom they identify as Gus, takes particular interest in young women, stopping to peer into their faces before disappearing in a mist. Apparently, Gus was so distraught after spotting his wife kissing another man during a stop in the village that he hanged himself from an oak tree, and now he walks the towpath searching for his faithless wife.

There are also the faint, fragmentary rumors of ghosts at Waterloo. Carl Zipper, who volunteers across the road at the Mount Allamuchy

The boatman hanged himself from an oak tree, they say, and now his ghost walks the towpath in search of his faithless wife. *Robert Oakes.*

Scout Reservation, told me, "I heard some years ago a story that one of the buildings [at Waterloo] was used as a hospital by the Continental army [during the Revolutionary War] and is purportedly haunted by one or more deceased soldiers. But unfortunately, I can't remember any particulars."

When I went to Waterloo that day, what I most hoped to find was someone with a firsthand account, but if the woodchuck and deer had seen anything strange, they certainly seemed unwilling to talk. Fortunately, after some online searching, I was able to track down two local residents with stories to share, Bob Parichuk and Al Amey.

A retired construction manager for the New Jersey State Park Service, Bob Parichuk said he experienced several unusual encounters while working at Waterloo. In the basement of the 1874 Peter D. Smith House, Bob said he was once accosted by a cold spot on a warm June day.

"There was no power running to the building, so it was pitch black in the basement," Bob recalled. "As I went down, it took a minute for my eyes to adjust....Then, out of nowhere, my light went out. It just totally died. So here I was in the pitch black, and my spare battery pack was in my truck."

So Bob felt his way out, got a new battery pack and ventured back down into the basement.

As I was going down the stairs, I turned to the right, and I felt a rush of cold air touch me on the back. And I stopped. It hit me. It wasn't like I walked into a colder area. It was like something was following close behind me down the stairs, and when I stopped, it ran into me. That's what it felt like. It was all over my back.

Bob then began taking pictures of the house. At the time, he said, he saw nothing unusual, but when he examined the photos carefully a few days later, he was shocked at what he found.

In the first one I took...I noticed something that looked like an orb. There were distinct markings. I didn't know how to explain it. That piqued my interest. So I started looking at the other ones, and sure enough...I saw the same thing: an orb, a distinct shape, round on top, straight on the sides and round on the bottom.

But it was what Bob saw in the last photo—depicting the front of the house with its many dark windows—that took his breath away. "I enlarged it and zeroed in on each window, and I came across one that looked like

Bob Parichuk and Al Amey spotted a face in one of the second-floor windows (*inset*) in this photo of the Peter D. Smith House. *Bob Parichuk.*

there was a little kid looking through it. I showed it to other people, and they said, 'Wow!'"

Friend and former coworker Al Amey, who has had his own strange experiences at Waterloo, said he saw something else in the photo.

Bob recalled: "When I showed it to Al, he said, 'What about the woman standing behind the boy?' So, I looked, and I thought, it does sort of look like a woman standing behind him with a high collar, her hair in a bun, and glasses on," Bob continued.

"It's a full apparition looking at you," Al said. "It's awesome!"

Bob said he once came upon an old photo posted to a social media site that showed a young woman who he believed resembled the woman in his photo. "I swear to God her hair and glasses match the figure in my photo." As the picture had been taken at Waterloo in the early 1900s, he wondered whether this could have been the same woman whose ghost he captured more than one hundred years later. As for the other apparition, "I have no idea who the boy might have been. But he is clear. The face is there."

Both Bob and Al said they have also experienced odd things in the Stagecoach Inn and Tavern, reportedly a hot spot of paranormal activity at the village.

The Stagecoach Inn and Tavern is reported to be a hot spot of paranormal activity at the village. *Robert Oakes.*

As I walked in the rain beside the old gristmill, ghosts of memories appeared to my mind's eye. *Robert Oakes.*

"The ghost in the tavern and the old hotel slammed doors when I was walking around," Al said. "It must be the tavern keeper or the bartender, because he slams stuff and he wants you out. He doesn't want you in there."

"Every time I go into the tavern, it's a weird atmosphere," said Bob, recalling one time when he entered the building to do some electrical work.

> *I was the only one in the building. I walked down the stairs…and right above me was the floor I came down from. I heard the sound you hear when someone steps on a board and it creaks. But I didn't hear anyone walking up to it, and it was not expansion from heat. It was like someone stepped on the board. I looked up and said, "Hello?" And there was nothing. But it was like someone was in the building. Other workers have experienced doors slamming shut. I can't verify those, but these are the stories people tell. It's the stuff you hear along the line.*

"Oh, there's plenty of action there," Al said.

But as I walked in the rain among those empty buildings, the only action I could see were the ghosts in a memory that suddenly appeared to my mind's eye. I was walking with a friend into the old gristmill. We were listening as someone shouted over the sound of rushing water, explaining to us how the wheel worked. Then we were in the old hotel and tavern. And I could smell the cloves and oranges they had set out in a bowl. A woman was in period clothing. And I was in another time.

I left Waterloo that day feeling happy to have seen it again after so many years and to have been reminded of those moments from my past and hoping it will live on for many more years to come to tell more tales of its ghosts.

CHAPTER 5

THE STANHOPE HOUSE

A s I walked through the door of the Stanhope House, out of a heavy downpour, I heard the jingle-jangle of an old upright piano, and I thought, *Now* that's *how you enter a legendary blues club.* But when I noticed that the piano was playing without any player I could see, I thought, *Now* that's *how you enter a legendary blues club that has its own resident ghosts, especially ones said to manifest in musical ways.* I imagine my host, general manager Ren Giliberti, had this in mind when he started up the antique pianola, knowing full well that I had not come there that night to hear one of the many famous blues artists who often grace the Stanhope House stage. That night, I was there to hear about the ghosts.

"I can't say I've had experiences here myself," Ren was quick to tell me while we watched the keys bounce as if pressed by invisible fingers, "but some of our employees have." And as you would expect, many of those experiences have involved the sound of singing. Once, he said, a man felt the air in the restroom suddenly turn ice cold as a female voice began to sing outside the door. Though the man couldn't make out any words, the voice was undeniable. In her 2008 book *Ghosthunting New Jersey*, L'Aura Hladik described similar experiences. According to Hladik, both the former owner, Maureen Myers, and her daughter, Mary, as well as the sound engineer, often heard a female voice singing as they stood in the sound booth, though no one was ever on stage at the time.

When I asked Ren again whether he had ever experienced anything like that at the club, he revealed, "At times when I'm alone late at night, usually

Out of a heavy downpour, I ventured into the haunted Stanhope House. *Robert Oakes.*

after midnight when I'm closing up, I get a feeling, and I want to get out of here. Now, is it just my own feeling, or is there really something there?" Ren said he wasn't sure, but as a self-described believer in the paranormal and the grandson of a psychic medium, he seemed quite open to the possibility.

Ren isn't alone in feeling that things become especially active late at night. That same sound engineer mentioned by Hladik also reported feeling uneasy whenever he had to close up by himself as the witching hour approached. And according to *Weird NJ*, a group of mediums and investigators once experienced a sudden storm of paranormal activity beginning at three o'clock in the morning that involved strange noises, the sound of backwards speech and strong readings on their detection devices. According to the report, one investigator that night even suffered scratches on his back.

As we continued to talk, Ren acknowledged that he may have actually seen something strange at the club one night, though he wasn't sure. "Once, while walking through the kitchen," he said, "I thought I saw a face in my periphery."

Actually, it's easy to see faces at the Stanhope House. The walls are lined with portraits of blues greats like Muddy Waters, Stevie Ray Vaughan, Debbie Davies and Buddy Guy, musical legends whose performances still resonate, soaked into the floorboards and the hand-hewn beams. Everywhere you look, you can see their faces smiling back at you. But I know that's not what he means.

He means an actual apparition like the one a bartender saw: the figure of a woman, reflected in the glass of a barroom door, gliding eerily behind her. He means shadow figures seen from the corner of an eye or the ghost of a woman passing through closed doors. He means the male ghost in a doorway and the female spirit near the mixing board that Maureen Myers described in an October 2000 *New York Times* article by Jillian Hornbeck Amroz or the wraithlike replay of two men fighting to the death—an event believed to have occurred there in the 1800s—once seen by a band member while performing onstage.

But the Stanhope House spirits haven't always been seen; their presence has also been detected in odd sounds or in the displacement of objects. According to Hladik, a handyman once discovered that his lost hammer had become inexplicably lodged under the bathroom floorboards. *Weird NJ* reported that a painter's scraper once moved on its own across a table, prompting two members of the painting crew to walk immediately off the job out of fear and superstition. And the one who did stay refused to work alone after that experience. There have been reports of doors opening and closing on their own, dirty glasses cleaned and put away, cocktail napkins placed on the bar and a soap dispenser operating on its own. And some have heard stairs creaking, the sound of footsteps on the upstairs floor and even what sounded like someone trying to get attention with a *psst, psst*.

So who might these spirits be? Some have identified one as the ghost of "George," a bartender who reportedly hanged himself in an upstairs room during the 1970s. In the *New York Times* report, Myers suggested that it may be the ghosts of previous owners who died in the building, while others point to an attic fire that once claimed the lives of ten to twenty people. At least one psychic medium claimed to sense the presence of a young child who was being held there against her will, and another felt that the spirits of formerly enslaved African Americans may linger in the basement, possibly having to do with the Underground Railroad. Also in the basement, some believe, is the spirit of an Italian immigrant who was hired long ago to stoke the coal furnace. And then, of course, there is the singing woman.

Because the Stanhope House has seen so many incarnations during its long history, it's really anybody's guess as to who may haunt it and out of what era they may come. Built as a family home in 1794, around the time the town of Stanhope was settled as a center of iron production, the building has served as a town hall, post office and jail; a library; a general store; a stagecoach stop along the Morris and Sussex Turnpike; a public house, where Daniel Webster was said to speak; a brothel (allegedly); a

I can't say for sure there wasn't a ghost pressing the keys of this antique pianola. *Robert Oakes.*

Prohibition speakeasy frequented by Babe Ruth; a rooming house; and a roadhouse tavern. Back in the days of the Morris Canal, the building also accommodated canal workers, providing a separate "puller's bar" exclusively for the smelly boatmen. And some claim that the history of the property extends even further back in time, having been deeded to a nobleman by the English king in 1752. A deep well beneath the floorboards, it is believed, is what remains of that early incarnation.

But it is as a rollicking music club with rustic decor and home-cooked meals that most people know and love the Stanhope House today. It was the Wrobleski family, back in the 1970s, who gave the building this new life. And ever since, it has been an off-the-beaten-track stop for traveling blues legends and an intimate hometown honkytonk for locals.

And, if the stories are true, for a few unseen guests, as well.

I myself didn't experience anything unusual at the Stanhope House that night, and as I said goodbye to Ren and thanked him for his hospitality, I felt just a little bit sad about that. But as I walked back out into the blustering storm, I took one last look at that old pianola, and I thought, *How do I know for sure there wasn't a ghost pressing on those keys?* After all, I hadn't actually seen Ren turn it on.

CHAPTER 6
STERLING HILL

THE HAUNTED MINE WITH A HEART OF GOLD

A s Bill Kroth, president of the Sterling Hill Mining Museum in Ogdensburg, sat down to speak with me about the ghosts of the mine, there was something he wanted to be sure I understood from the start.

"I am an engineer. That field is totally based upon science," he said. "I don't believe in this."

Then, just as I thought the interview was over, he added, "But I have seen things here that are beyond belief."

So I leaned in a little bit closer. *What have you seen?* I wondered.

"People have seen orbs and figures made of black smoke. They hear things, names spoken and voices from deep in the mine."

Someone once spotted a phantom face peering through the window just beside where we were sitting. Psychics sense the resonance of a tragic accident in the East Shaft. And some tour guides refuse to venture into the mines at night, afraid of what they'll hear or feel while alone in there.

"There's definitely something going on here," Bill said. "This is the real deal."

But what about Bill? I wondered. *What has he experienced?*

I once saw a "lady in white" in our Geo-Tech Building. It was early in the morning, and my wife and I were the only ones on the property. My wife was working over in the office, and I was the only one in the building. First, I heard a faint whisper for about thirty seconds; it seemed about ten feet away from me towards the central part of the room. Then I saw the figure, only for a split second, but I saw it. I will admit that I quickly left without grabbing my tools.

But that experience didn't stop Bill from staying overnight in the same building once while doing some maintenance work. And that night, he said, he heard something up on the second floor.

I had put a new coat of polyurethane on the floor of the board room upstairs, and I had just gone to bed downstairs when I started hearing footsteps up there. The room was locked, and there was caution tape to keep people from walking on the floor. So I went upstairs, ready to kill whoever I found. But there was no one there, and there were no footprints on the floor.

On the surface, Bill's affirmation of the Sterling Hill ghosts, in spite of his scientific skepticism, might seem like a contradiction. But it may be that there are certain things that can't be proven or disproven by science. They can only be experienced on some level deep inside.

As Bill put it, "When you come here and you see things and you hear things, that's the proof. It's not about belief."

And with that, the interview was over. What more was there to say? We could talk all day about the mine and its ghosts, but that wouldn't bring me closer to experiencing them. I had to get immersed. I had to feel it for myself. And to do that, I had to take the next tour, just then assembling outside.

"Let's go," Bill said as he walked to the door. And I clicked my pen and followed him.

Outside, Bill introduced me to Ken, our guide, who led us first into the Zobel Hall Museum, at one time the miners' changing room, where the clothing they once wore hung like ghosts above their lockers. I seemed to be the only one who was there to hear about the hauntings, though. So after his official introduction, Ken set the group loose to explore the hall on their own and then pulled me aside to talk about ghosts.

"You come in here at night, and you hear things," he said. "You hear clanging, like a metallic sound. I haven't heard voices, because I'm usually with other people. But there's no question: I have heard sounds. And it makes your hair stand up on end."

Ken said he has gone looking for the spirits. "I'm very curious about it. I go in sometimes and turn off all the lights. I want to see something." But all he has ever seen has turned out to be natural phenomena. "I've seen mists form, but it's a mine. You get that in there. It doesn't take much for the imagination, especially when you're alone. But if anyone's going to see a ghost, it's in this mine."

Ken said he doesn't especially like it when he hears the metallic sounds, but the ghosts don't frighten him, unlike someone he once worked with, who was alarmed to feel the tap of something unseen as he stood on top of a stepladder.

"I said, 'You're a ghost magnet, young man. But don't be afraid, they just want your attention. They're curious.'"

Ken told me about the Geo-Tech Building, an especially active location where psychics often sense vibrations and many others have claimed to hear voices. Another common report, he said, is the appearance of phantom workmen walking into the mine.

Before we left the Zobel Hall Museum, Ken brought me to the locker that once belonged to a miner named John Kolic, now decorated as a shrine to his memory. From 1972 until his death in 2014, John devoted himself to Sterling Hill, first as a miner and later as a member of the museum's staff. Ken told me about John's love for the place, of how he salvaged many minerals as the tunnels gradually filled with water, resulting in many new discoveries, including one, Kolicite, that was named in his honor.

Said Ken, "John lived and loved the mine. If anyone is to come through, it would be him. He wanted to be here and nowhere else. If anyone is going to haunt this place, it's John."

And sure enough, sometime after John's death, Bill himself reported hearing John's gravelly voice in the mine.

At last, with my mind full of ghost stories, it was time to enter the mine. And as we walked toward the green metal door that opened into the rock face, I was told about yet another spirit. Beside the path was an old red bike said to belong to a former miner nicknamed Bicycle Pete. In life, Pete rode the bike to work each morning until the day he fell to his death. Now, they say, his ghost haunts the place, often seen riding his trademark bike.

Nearing the door, I was also introduced to board member Doug Francisco, a former miner who once worked with John Kolic. As he walked beside me, Doug shared his impressions of the man and his love for the mine.

John called it his home. After the mine was closed and sealed with concrete, the new owners reopened the mine by breaking through that seal. John, being

One of the spirits said to haunt the mine is known as Bicycle Pete. People claim to see the phantom miner riding his trademark bike. *Robert Oakes.*

> *the first person to reenter the mine after almost four years, said "I'm home."*
> *He loved this place, and he liked to be here alone.*

Doug told me that, while he himself has never had paranormal experiences, it doesn't mean he doesn't believe. "There's a difference," he said. When I asked if it ever bothered him to work so deep underground with so many tons of rock above his head, he said no. "You learn to respect it," as I myself was about to do.

Mining at Sterling Hill and nearby Franklin began in the 1700s with the early Dutch settlers, who initially expected to find copper and iron in these hills. After zinc was found to be the predominant mineral, a number of companies were established to extract it, ultimately leading to the foundation of the New Jersey Zinc Company in 1897, which operated here until 1986, making it the last of the Sussex County mines. Before it was shut down and flooded, Sterling Hill consisted of thirty-five miles of tunnels reaching to a depth of 2,675 feet. When it was reopened as a museum in the early 1990s, only the surface level of the mine remained accessible to the public.

But as I stepped out of the sunlight and into the cold, damp darkness, surface level felt deep enough for me.

We walked the long, straight tunnel that lay before us until it turned into a passage twisting deep into the mountain. Ken pointed out the formation of new limestone on the surface of the rough, ancient rock, carried down by water dripping from ceiling to floor. One drop tapped me on the head. *Not a ghost*, I told myself. But as the last person in the group, I felt it was my duty to turn and check whether those were more drops I'd heard or whether something was scuttling up behind us in the mist.

We reached a fenced area where mannequins of miners were placed to help us imagine the kind of work that had been done there years ago. Someone called a "grizzly man" was in charge of sending rocks down a deep hole through a sieve, where they would be pulverized in a crusher. Any rocks that didn't fit through the sieve had to be pushed through with a pole. It was

Was something scuttling up behind us in the mist, or was it only the sound of water drips? *Robert Oakes.*

The candle made our shadows move along the walls. *Robert Oakes.*

a grueling job, and dangerous. It wasn't unheard of for a grizzly man to fall to a grisly death.

As we walked into the shaft station, a high ceiling opened above us. Here, Ken showed us where the miners used to stand shoulder to shoulder on the narrow elevator that brought them down to one of the nineteen levels below. I knew those tunnels were now flooded, but that didn't keep me from thinking that I'd heard something down there. Maybe a voice or maybe a rumble—whatever it was, it sounded like it had come from a deep and cavernous place.

Ken told me that the shaft station is often highly active during the many paranormal investigations that take place in the mine. Pointing toward the metal struts and platforms that were bolted to the high ceiling, he said, "They see things in those catwalks."

What things? I wondered. But we were already on to the next location.

At the end of a long corridor, Ken warned us that things were about to get dark. To simulate the detonations once used to break open new passageways, Ken shut the lights off and played a recording of a warning whistle followed by an explosion. After standing for a moment in the utter dark, I was grateful for the candle Ken lit, though it made our shadows move along the walls.

A dance of electrons can make cold stones come alive with light, just like the spirits of the dead. *Robert Oakes.*

But it was the light of the fluorescent rocks that took my breath away. As we moved slowly through the darkened chamber, we caught the ghostly greens and reds and blues of what had seemed like cold, dead stones. Under a blacklight, they came alive with an inner luminescence and seemed to radiate heat.

"Our rock is famous for fluorescence," Ken told us. "Scientists come from all around the world to study it."

And I could understand why; it was an amazing thing to see. Even after a billion years, even down in the dark depths, far from the reach of the sun, a dance of electrons can make a cold body come alive with light.

Just like the spirits of the dead, I thought.

We made our way back out into the sun; I had made it through the mine without experiencing something I could be certain was a ghost. Nevertheless, I certainly experienced something—something I didn't expect. I expected the mine to feel cold and dank, but I was surprised to find a warm radiance in the dark. I thought about how John Kolic called the mine his home, how he wanted to be there more than anywhere else in the world and how he saved so many of its minerals from the flood. And then suddenly it came to me. Wasn't it John's spirit I had met in the mine? Isn't it his watchful presence that gives the place its warmth, along with the passion and dedication that all those who care for it now clearly feel?

I went into that cold, dark place looking for the dead, and I found instead a warm, beating heart of gold.

CHAPTER 7

THE HAUNTED VAPOR ROOM

I expected the proprietors of a place called the Haunted Vapor Room to have a ghost story or two to tell, and owner Cindy Barton did not disappoint. Not only did she share with me many incidents of paranormal activity in her 1797 home in Franklin, which currently houses the vape and CBD shop, but she also told me who she believes the spirit to be.

"We think it's Sam Munson," a former state senator, whose family owned the home and the farm that once surrounded it for more than 150 years. The same Sam Munson who died in 1961 and is buried in nearby Hardyston Cemetery.

"He's been seen right here," Cindy told me, as she pointed to the stairwell at the back of the entrance hall. "Everybody sees him…and he's always dressed in black pants and a white shirt." Everybody sees him, that is, except for Cindy.

"I try to see him all the time, but I never have," she said. "I've looked in the basement. I've looked in the attic. Nothing. I've never seen anything."

Though she may not have laid eyes on the Munson House ghost, Cindy believes she has encountered it. Early on, she said, when she and her husband, Pat, first purchased the property, she often sensed an unseen presence. And it wasn't long before the spirit began to pull pranks.

"Things would go missing," she said, recalling her first strange experience.

I was putting up Christmas lights. I set up a table in the middle of the floor and put twine, scissors and the lights on it. I was going back and forth into

A place called the Haunted Vapor Room is bound to have some resident ghosts. *Robert Oakes.*

the kitchen, and I came back in, and the scissors were gone. And I'm like, "Okay, I must have left them out there." So I went out, and the scissors weren't there. So I looked all over. And I'm like, "C'mon, where are they?" Then I go back in, and they're sitting in the middle of the table. And I'm like, "They freaking weren't there!" And that's what used to happen to me all the time. They would mess with me like that.

Another time, Cindy said, the spirit somehow moved a vacuum. "I was vacuuming, and I went in the other room and came back and it was gone. And I'm like, 'It's a freaking vacuum! How did you hide a vacuum? You're a ghost. Where did you put it?'"

After looking in closets and the upstairs rooms, Cindy said she returned to find the vacuum sitting just where she had left it before it went missing.

"And I'm like, 'You're kidding me, right?' But that's the kind of thing that happened to me. They were just messing with me, like it was a joke."

Cindy said she began to tell the spirits to knock it off.

"I'd just start saying to them, 'Seriously, I don't have time for this. Put it back.' And I would go do something else, and then it would be back.'"

After enough of these experiences, Cindy began to demand that the ghost show itself.

"I'd walk all through the house, and I'd be like, 'C'mon, where are you?'" But the ghost has yet to appear to her.

Her husband, Pat, though, whom Cindy described as a "complete non-believer," has seen it. Early on, when Cindy would tell Pat about the odd experiences she'd had, he would dismiss any notion of ghosts. "My husband was like, 'Yeah, it's all bullshit. Whatever.'" But late one night, as Pat was pulling away from the back of the building in his truck, he spotted a face peering out through a window in the stairwell, a window that sits about eight feet from the floor, which means that if someone were peering through it, they'd have to be…

"Yeah, they'd have to be hovering," said Cindy. "So, then he called me and he's like, 'Who's in the building? I just saw somebody in the window.' And I'm like, 'Go back and see who it is.'" When Pat flatly refused to reenter the building, Cindy asked, "Well, who did you see?" To which, Pat replied, "I think I saw the ghost."

Since having this experience, Pat's opinion on the matter has shifted.

"He knows it's haunted," Cindy said, and he will not venture into the building alone late at night, as Cindy sometimes does.

"He's like, 'You're crazy.' And I'm like, 'It's a ghost. Obviously, if they wanted to hurt us, we'd be dead. Clearly, they're not malevolent.'"

Instead, Cindy believes the spirit to be watchful and protective. "Whatever's here is good, that's what I feel."

But a benevolent ghost is still a ghost and can still cause quite a shock, like the time their son came bounding down the stairs in two leaps after spotting the spirit on the second floor.

"And he's like, 'Mom, there's somebody up there.' And I said, 'Who's up there? What is wrong with you?' And he goes, 'No, Mom. It's something… different. I could see through him.' And I said, 'Show me.' So we went upstairs, but there was nothing there." When asked to describe the spirit, her son said what everybody else says: black pants and a white, long-sleeved, button-down shirt.

Though this ghost may be the most prominent one in the house, it may not be the only one; there may also be the ghost of a playful child.

"When we first bought it, I had Thanksgiving here and the whole place was empty," Cindy said. "My niece, who was three years old at the time, was upstairs playing, and then she came down." Cindy asked her niece what she was doing up there, and she replied, "I'm playing with the little girl."

Two women who once owned a gift shop on the second floor may also have experienced frequent encounters with this little girl ghost. "They sold toys," Cindy explained, "and they would come in, and all the toys would be on the floor in the middle of the room, all set up like there were kids up there playing." What made this all the more amazing was the fact that the gift shop owners had always kept their doors locked at night with a deadbolt.

And the encounters with child spirits have not been limited to the second floor; things have also been reported in the basement.

> *We went down one day, and there were children's bare footprints on the concrete floor. They were white, and they started in the middle of the room and then just ended. And they looked like they were chalk or paint. So, I'm like, "All right, who's the idiot that did it?" I checked with everybody, and everybody said no.*

Cindy said she tried to remove the prints with paint thinner or by scratching at them, but nothing worked. "They were there for two weeks, and everybody that worked here saw them. Then I came in one day, and they were completely gone—like, disappeared, gone. It was weird. And everybody here just assumed it was the ghost."

Some local plumbers hired by the Bartons were reluctant to take on the job because they had heard the place was haunted, Cindy said. "And these were like big, huge guys, and my husband's like, 'Are you kidding me?' So they came over to work, and they were in the basement. And I came over here, and there was music blasting down there. And I said to my husband, 'Why are they blasting the music?' And Pat said, 'They blasted the music so they didn't hear the kids laughing in the basement.'"

While some locals and the occasional customer may be wary of the old Munson House, Cindy is quick to reassure them. "If there was anything to be afraid of, I'd tell you," she said. "I wouldn't still be here. But it's never been anything bad."

In fact, the Bartons celebrate their ghosts. Years ago, when they ran a café on the premises, they included firsthand accounts of unusual encounters on the front page of their menu. And every October, they host a big Halloween party with food and live music in the gazebo.

As Cindy led me through the rooms, I could feel her love for this historic property. "It's just a cool old house, and I love old houses. And I love hauntings. I love all that stuff. And I think older places are where the ghosts are, because why would they be in a new place? If somebody dies in a place,

Exploring the attic of the old Munson House. *Robert Oakes.*

and they're going to be a ghost, where else would they go but back to where they knew?" And so it stands to reason that at least one of the Munson House ghosts might be Samuel Munson himself. Who the child may be is still anybody's guess.

For all her belief and enthusiasm, Cindy still awaits the day when she can see the ghosts with her own eyes. In the meantime, she can at least feel relieved that they no longer want to pull pranks on her. "They don't bother me anymore. They don't hide things. I think they're either just used to me, or they're happy. I don't know. I don't know why ghosts do what they do."

CHAPTER 8

THE CAVE GRAVE OF NEWTON
AND WHAT MAY LIE BENEATH

I f I hadn't seen it myself in a photograph, I might not have believed it. But there it was: a stone tablet set in a rock face at the back of the Newton Cemetery, inscribed with the names James W., Margaret M. and J. Howard Lewis and the date 1909. I had heard that the names belong to three children who had wandered underground through a hole in the rock and were later declared dead, though their bodies were never found. To honor their memory and to prevent a repeat of the tragedy, it was said, the town sealed the hole with the tablet.

What made the story seem suspect to me was the fact that I could find no mention of it in the newspaper archives. How could that be? When, in 1982, forty-eight-year-old Scoutmaster Donald Weltner died in nearby Lafayette after two days trapped in Crooked Swamp Cave, the incident was reported all over the country. But three young children go missing in the limestone caverns under Newton, and the papers have nothing to say? I found that hard to believe. Also, according to *Weird NJ*, the Sussex County Historical Society has almost no record of this event. Apparently, all that is documented is that three children are indeed buried at the site.

Regardless of the lack of written records, the story of the cave grave has deep roots in Newton, known to many who live there. One local man I spoke with knew exactly where it was and told me all he knew about the story. He also told me that he once saw an odd figure standing in the path that leads to the Lewis grave.

The story of the cave grave has deep roots in Newton, known to many who live there. *Katherine Oakes.*

This man isn't the only local resident to report seeing something strange in that location. One contributor to *Weird NJ* told of how he and some friends went to investigate the sound of cracking sticks beside the rock face one night, only to run scared when they saw a little girl in dirty clothes holding her neck as if she couldn't breathe. He later wondered whether it was the ghost of young Margaret Lewis they had seen that night.

Numerous posts on social media sites show just how well known the cave grave tale is. Commenter after commenter shares memories of hearing it told to them by a relative or of passing the stone on their daily walk to school, while others engage in a vigorous debate about the tale's authenticity. One commenter even shared a story of something demonic lurking deep within the cave.

This commenter is not the only one to tell tales of dark things dwelling in tunnels under Newton. In his book *New Jersey Haunts,* Elias Zwillenberg writes of the passageways that are believed to lie beneath the downtown and of entities said to inhabit them. According to Zwillenberg, local lore has it that a number of the buildings downtown are haunted by spirits that enter from the tunnels below, including those of children that peer through air vents and that of a man in a top hat.

At the Newton Fire Museum on Spring Street, it is the ghost of former curator Howard "Blackie" Blackwell that is said to linger. According to an article by Cristy Carlson in the October 5, 2018 edition of the *New Jersey Herald*, Blackie watches over the historic red brick building and makes his presence known through the scent of apple pipe tobacco and the occasional good-natured prank.

While none of the reports about Blackie have him emerging from the tunnels below, in *Sussex County Hauntings*, author Eleanor Wagner tells of another Spring Street building that may be haunted by subterranean spirits. After renovation of the property exposed an entrance to the underground tunnels, Wagner writes, the proprietor began to experience supernatural torments, including violent knocking, disembodied screams and objects being thrown across the room.

It is interesting to note that Spring Street was apparently once the scene of many public executions. According to the 1846 book *Historical Collections of the State of New Jersey* by John Barber and Henry Howe, "What is now called Spring Street…was formerly called the Gallows Road, on account of a number having been hung along that road."

If the stories are true about the many tunnels under Newton, then where did they come from, and why are they there? Some say they were built by bootleggers during Prohibition, while others link them to the Underground Railroad. Some say they were used as service entrances for downtown businesses. And still others—like old-timers who talk about walking through them from town to town or crossing an underground pond by boat—say they simply offered a cool way to travel in the heat of the day. Some even claim to have driven through them by car!

Actually, it's not unusual to find underground passageways in this part of New Jersey, some man-made and others naturally occurring. Hundreds of abandoned mines, pits, shafts and tunnels testify to the region's long history of metal and mineral extraction, which began in the 1600s with the early Dutch along the Delaware, continued through the eighteenth and nineteenth centuries at sites like nearby Andover and ended with the closure of the Sterling Hill Mine in Ogdensburg in 1986.

There are also naturally occurring caves, rock shelters and limestone caverns lining the landscape in these higher elevations, some that are considered to be archaeologically significant because of the Indigenous artifacts found inside.

According to local lore, some of these caves and rock shelters are also connected to legendary figures and events. At Big Muckshaw Pond in Fredon Township, for example, a place called Moody's Rock and its surrounding swamps are said to have been the Revolutionary War hideout of Lieutenant

James Moody, a Sussex County farmer turned Loyalist spy and marauder. A great deal of lore surrounds Moody and his rock, under which, it is said, he hid gold now guarded by his ghost. In *Historical Collections*, Barber and Howe described the haunted scene as

> *in many places abounding in stagnant pools, and noxious weeds, or foul swampy shrubs, very difficult, if not totally impossible to be traversed....* *To the southward it runs off into a ridge of irregular rocks, thickly shaded by a dense growth of trees, which for many a long year have concealed the gloomy haunts within...gloomy woods, dark defiles, misshapen crags, and a wild and dismal scenery.*

It has been said that Moody was able to access a broad network of tunnels from this spot, some that stretched as far as a mile away to a cave called the Devil's Den (or Devil's Hole) in Newton, which was described as "a deep hole with a long subterranean passage attached to it" by Max Schrabisch in his 1915 book *Indian Habitations in Sussex County, New Jersey.* But a state report filed by geologist Richard F. Dalton in 1976 contradicts any notion that this passage stretches as far as Moody's Rock. In his report on the Devil's Den, Dalton writes, though "a legend about the cave says that it continues for a mile...like most legends about the size of caves, this one is greatly exaggerated; there are no negotiable passages in any direction from the cave."

But government reports and academic studies never stop people from telling tales, tales that are well worth preserving because they give us much more than the facts. They give us what people remember, what they hope for and what they fear or what they wonder and imagine. They also express the presence of a place, what it feels like to be there. The story of the three lost Lewis children gives us Newton's remembrance, while the tales of ghosts in the tunnels and caves give us its sense of something lurking in the deep. Certainly, the wealth of lore about the Sussex underground proves that metal isn't the only thing of value in these hills.

CHAPTER 9

ON THE TRAIL
OF THE WHITE PILGRIM

Tracking an old story can be a tricky task. In the various versions that exist, details can become confused; names, dates and locations can be lost or changed. With no story that I have explored for this book have I found that to be truer than with this, the story of the White Pilgrim. Granted, it was a confusing tale to begin with, even without the passage of time making matters even more murky. It involved three different locations for the same church congregation, three different graveyards and an itinerant minister who was hard to pin down in life, let alone in the afterlife.

As I planned an excursion through the Warren County towns where this was all said to have taken place, I reached out to one of my oldest friends, Jared, to ask if he would come along. Jared's a scientist at Rutgers, and he's probably the most analytical thinker I know. But more than that, as kids back in the '80s, Jared and I would spend endless summer days untangling the mysteries of lore and mythology over the jangling sounds of *Super Mario Brothers*. And later, endless evenings were given over to delving into Dungeons & Dragons or exploring the arcana of Cthulhu. Who else but Jared could help me unravel such a mystery?

Before setting out that day, I did some research, starting with the writings of Henry Charlton Beck. Back in 1964, Beck noted the winding road down which old lore can take you, often leading to unintended ends. He had come to this same area to explore the local lore, but at first, it seems he wasn't interested in the White Pilgrim. He was drawn there instead to look for towns no longer found on modern maps, to explore the mystery of a missing milestone marker, said to be one of the oldest objects in the county, and to learn more about an old pig drover who once told stories on the back porch of a Johnsonburg hotel. But Beck heard rumors about the Pilgrim from some of the old-timers he spoke to, and he was eventually led to a certain Elizabeth Cool, who was in possession of a newspaper clipping that told the Pilgrim's tale, as well as the lyrics to a lament for the minister that Mrs. Cool recalled her grandmother singing. Beck was also led to where the Yellow Frame Presbyterian Church had once stood beside the Dark of the Moon Graveyard. This graveyard, like the road that winds around it, was apparently named after a nearby inn whose sign, according to *Pioneer Families of Northwestern New Jersey* by William C. Armstrong, featured a dark crescent moon on a light-colored background.

By then, Beck was hard on the trail of the White Pilgrim, whether or not he knew it, for it was in that eighteenth-century burying ground that the body of Joseph Thomas, a traveling minister from Ohio—known as the White Pilgrim on account of the colorless garments he wore—was said to have been buried in 1835 after succumbing to smallpox. By the time Beck arrived, though, Thomas's body was no longer there, as it had been moved eleven years after its initial burial to the Johnsonburg Christian Cemetery, where it remains to this day beneath a white stone obelisk. At no point, apparently, had his body ever been interred near the present-day Yellow Frame Church, which was built in 1887 in Fredon Township on the Warren-Sussex border, some miles away from the Dark of the Moon. And yet, stories persist that his ghost haunts that church. Or is it that he haunted the previous Yellow Frame Church, built in 1786, which once stood among the tombstones across the street? Or does his spirit linger in the Johnsonburg cemetery where his body actually lies, or does it haunt the place where it once lay, the now-abandoned Dark of the Moon Burying Ground, the original site of the Yellow Frame Church, known then as Upper Hardwick Church?

Confused yet? Good. Now you know how I felt. Maybe it will help to clear things up if I back up now and tell the tale, at least as I have come to understand it. And if I myself mistake any facts, I hope you'll forgive me. As I said, this White Pilgrim is hard to pin down.

Born in North Carolina in 1790, Joseph Thomas was the ninth child of a wealthy, generous father and an attentive, affectionate mother. When he was seven years old, however, his family lost their wealth, forcing his parents to send the young boy off to live with strangers who mistreated him, putting him to menial work instead of enrolling him in school. During those years, Thomas found solace in the two books his father had given him, one of

Did the Pilgrim's ghost haunt the old Yellow Frame Church that once stood among the tombstones across the street from the present-day church? *Robert Oakes.*

which was the Bible. At the age of nine, he went to live with one of his brothers, who entered him into school, where he began to progress swiftly. It was then that an event occurred that would forever alter the course of his life. While he was bedridden with a debilitating illness, the house Thomas was in caught fire. As the flames spread all around him, he commended himself to God's protection and vowed that if he were allowed to escape, he would dedicate his life to preaching the Gospel. When the flames subsided, leaving him untouched, Thomas was born again into a new life of service to God. While still quite young, he entered the Christian ministry and began to preach. His early attempts were weak, and he was often discouraged and ridiculed, nicknamed "the Boy Preacher." Preachers of all denominations denounced him, calling him "Crazy Thomas," and even his own mother became mortified by her son's pious activity. Determined, Thomas deepened his study and developed his oratory skills, and soon people were coming from far and wide to hear him preach.

At that time, Thomas renounced his worldly possessions and set off on foot or horseback, at first staying close to home and later venturing into the

West and up into the Northeast. Traveling difficult and dangerous paths through the wilderness and often suffering insults and persecution, Thomas kept his promise to God to spread the Gospel to all who would listen. And everywhere he went, many were inspired by his eloquence and sincerity. After hearing him speak, some even converted on the spot. During this period, Thomas threw off his worldly clothes and began to dress entirely in white. Even his boots, hat, saddlebags and horse were now the color of milky chalk. Some said it was an expression of the purity of his soul; others said he believed it protected him against the evils of the world and inoculated him against disease. Still others said he wore the white simply to get attention. Whatever the reason, his unusual appearance certainly did enhance his reputation and garnered him a new and lasting nickname, the White Pilgrim.

While Thomas did marry, ultimately settling in Ohio with his wife, Christiana, and their four children, he never stopped his wanderings, continuing to suffer hardships for the sake of his vocation. In 1835, as he traveled east on a mission to New York City, the itinerant minister contracted smallpox; unbeknownst to him, he was infected when he later came to Johnsonburg to preach at the Episcopal church. Hours after he gave his sermon there, on April 9, 1835, the White Pilgrim fell ill and died.

As the story goes, community leaders chose to bury the Pilgrim's body in the distant Dark of the Moon Burying Ground out of fear of spreading the virulent contagion. Because the Presbyterian congregation that first established that graveyard in 1763 had since moved across the street from its current location in Fredon Township (present-day Yellow Frame Church), it seemed safe to bury the contaminated body in the disused graveyard.

Eleven years later, apparently after townspeople felt that there was no longer any danger of contamination, the remains of the White Pilgrim were moved to the Johnsonburg Christian Cemetery beneath the obelisk made of white Italian marble that bears this inscription: "Joseph Thomas, Minister of the Gospel in the Christian Church. Known as The White Pilgrim by reason of his wearing white raiment. Died April 9, 1835, aged 44 yrs, 1 mo. & 2 d's."

The White Pilgrim's wanderings and tragic death far from his home and family inspired Elder John Ellis to write what Beck called one of only a few intact early New Jersey folk songs, the lament that Beck's informant, Mrs. Cool, remembered her grandmother singing. Beck was unfamiliar with the melody and didn't ask Mrs. Cool if she could sing it for him, but many know the tune today, as it has been recorded by a range of musical artists, including Bob Dylan, who released his version as "The Lone Pilgrim" in 1993. The song begins:

> *I came to the spot where the White Pilgrim lay,*
> *And pensively stood by his tomb;*
> *When in a low whisper I heard something say—*
> *How sweetly I sleep here alone.*

Looking at the lyrics, I would call this a ghost story. After all, the speaker, while standing at the grave, suddenly hears the disembodied voice of the one who lies below. That certainly sounds to me like an account of paranormal activity.

In his own account, Beck made no mention of a ghost. However, many others have reported sightings. According to *Weird NJ*, not long after the Pilgrim's death, residents said they saw his spirit abroad throughout the region, sitting astride a white horse. The belief at the time was that the pious Pilgrim was angry at being buried in the forsaken cemetery, now more associated with the debauchery of the tavern than with the sanctity of the church. Apparently, once his remains were moved to the Christian cemetery, the sightings became less frequent.

But other reports suggest that the Pilgrim's ghost remained active even after reinterment. According to *The Big Book of New Jersey Ghost Stories* by Martinelli and Stansfield, Thomas's ghost has been seen on especially dark nights lurking in the Johnsonburg Christian Cemetery.

In *Ghosthunting New Jersey*, L'Aura Hladik mentions the belief of some that the Pilgrim's ghost haunts the present-day Yellow Frame Church, even though that building did not exist when he was buried in 1835 or even when his remains were reinterred in 1846, nor was he ever buried at that location. Nevertheless, some have reported the sound of unearthly organ music, doors flying open on their own, the sound of disembodied footsteps through fallen leaves and lights flickering on and off. And the suggestion, at least, is that the ghost of the White Pilgrim was behind these odd occurrences. Hladik herself photographed orbs in the Yellow Frame Cemetery and said that while there, she felt the presence of spirits all around her. Dennis William Hauck, in *Haunted Places: The National Directory*, also attributes the sound of eerie organ music and the flickering of lights at the Yellow Frame Church to the ghost of the White Pilgrim, which, Hauck reports, becomes especially active around Halloween. And while, in *Sussex County Hauntings*, author Eleanor Wagner does mention that some people pin the hauntings of

Not long after the White Pilgrim's death, residents said they saw his spirit abroad sitting astride a milky white horse. *Katherine Oakes.*

the Yellow Frame Church on the White Pilgrim, she goes on to tell of many reported occurrences at the church that may have nothing at all to do with the preacher's ghost.

Having gathered as much information as I could about the White Pilgrim, the Yellow Frame Church and the Dark of the Moon Burying Ground, I was eager to visit and see what I might see. It was a raw October afternoon when I met Jared and his wife, Evelyn, outside the Yellow Frame Church. With my hatchback open to block the intermittent rain, I shared with them some of what I had learned. Under umbrellas, we looked into the cemetery, established in 1786, appreciating the poignant beauty of its old stones. Looking out over the nearby fields, I could understand why the Presbyterian congregation was drawn up here to this location, far from the Dark of the Moon. Elevated on a ridge between two valleys, the Yellow Frame Church commands a stunning view of the surrounding countryside. And when the sun burst through the passing clouds, its bright, bold yellow siding answered like a signal fire.

With no sign here of the White Pilgrim, we drove down along Route 94 to the Johnsonburg Christian Cemetery, where we knew, at least, his grave was, if not also his ghost. From outside the iron gate, our eyes were drawn immediately to the white stone obelisk standing slightly tilted in the center of the cemetery. We realized that the obelisk had actually moved a little on its pedestal, which conjured up images of a restless spirit's attempted escape. The shivers that that thought gave us only increased when we looked around and realized that many of the stones had shifted in some way or that the graves themselves had sunk. At least one especially thick stone lay horizontally on the ground with a gap that had formed around its edge, partially exposing an opening into the earth below.

From outside the iron gate, our eyes were drawn to the white stone obelisk standing slightly tilted in the center of the cemetery. *Robert Oakes.*

The Pilgrim's grave is far from the others. Did they think his remains could still spread smallpox eleven years after his death? *Robert Oakes.*

"You can understand why people years ago might have seen something like that and imagined that the dead were rising from their graves," Jared observed. "They didn't know much about weathering and erosion."

And we wondered, did they place that especially heavy slab over the grave to keep the undead underground?

Looking back toward the Pilgrim's grave, Evelyn noticed how far it was from the others, seemingly a sign that they still feared the smallpox that killed him.

"Did they really think his remains could still spread the contagion eleven years after his death?" I wondered aloud. "And anyway, all of these people were already dead."

"They knew very little about germ theory back then," Jared noted.

Taking out my phone, I loaded up Dylan's "The Lone Pilgrim" and hit play. And as the words rang out near the Pilgrim's lonely stone, I hoped it let him know his life still meant something to us today. We couldn't help but wonder whether Thomas felt forsaken in the end. The same God who had rescued him from that burning house when he was a boy, who carried him through so many trials, didn't save him, at last, from the virus. Even as faithful a servant as the Pilgrim "met the contagion and sunk in the tomb," as the song says. Why? Was this a just reward for so much sacrifice and devotion? In the last words of the lament, Thomas seemed to offer a comforting answer: "The same hand that led me through scenes dark and drear has kindly conducted me home." And if his spirit is indeed at home with God, was there any chance we'd find him here?

Leaving the Johnsonburg Christian Cemetery, we made for Dark Moon Road. We expected the eighteenth-century burying ground to be much more difficult to find, and we were not wrong. We overshot and took a few wrong turns, but we eventually arrived at what we believed to be its general location. However, we also realized that whatever remains of it now appears to lie on private property, so we ended our search more than a little disappointed.

Just then, though, a man who lived in a neighboring house gave us a friendly wave that lifted our spirits. And as we chatted with him, we told him about the White Pilgrim, the old burying ground and the tavern that gave his street its name. He told us he had never heard this history, but now he was curious and wanted to know more. He said he'd heard that his house had been a tavern at one point, and he wondered whether it might have been the Dark Moon. I thought that was doubtful given what Beck observed in 1964, that all that remained of the old structure was the ghost of a cellar hole. But I loved that this man was beginning to wonder about the personal connection he may have to these legends. And I loved it when he shared with me some of his own local ghost stories, which I had never heard before.

There beside one of my oldest friends, talking lore with one of my newest, I could feel what Beck had once called "the true satisfaction which comes when this insatiable curiosity about what used to be develops new friendships, even reunions of family or old friends, for which no formal plans were made." It was such a joy to feel this connection over old stories and to share in a sense of wonder about the history and mysteries that surround us.

Despite all our wanderings that day, we did not see the ghost of the elusive White Pilgrim. Nevertheless, it was well worth the search. It was a moment to immerse ourselves in the lore and landscape of a beautiful part of New Jersey and to be reminded of why we must keep these old stories alive.

And as for the discrepancies over where the ghost may be found, who knows? Maybe the Pilgrim haunts each and every one. After all, he was a wandering spirit in life. Why not also in death? And maybe, as we wandered the countryside seeking contact with the unseen and a meaningful connection to our fellow man, the ghost of the White Pilgrim was made manifest in us.

CHAPTER 10

Northwestern New Jersey's Roadside Ghosts

P ositioned as it is amid the major city centers of the Northeast, New Jersey has long been a hub of transportation, a way to pass from one place to another. From the earliest days to modern times, footpaths and stagecoach roads, canals and railroads, city streets and interstates have been woven like a web across its terrain. And long before Bruce was born to run, Jerseyans have seen the road as both a place to get stuck and a way to get free. But in New Jersey, a road can also be a place to get scared—terrified—by any one of a number of roadside ghosts. Shades of Death Road and Clinton Road, both often included on lists of the most haunted roads in America, are just two of the places where the Jersey dead are said to walk in traffic.

Shades of Death Road

What gives a place a haunted reputation? Does it start with a story of an unusual encounter passed along by word of mouth? Is it an uncanny atmosphere unique to that location that inspires a sense of the unseen? Or does it all stem from a name, a name like Shades of Death? Certainly, you would expect such a place to have a few resident spirits, and indeed, many tales have been told about this Warren County road. But how much of this lore is invented, inspired by an evocative name, and how much is based on actual experiences?

Under low limbs and a violet sky, I peered into the darkness at the edge of my headlights, wondering what might appear beyond the next bend. *Robert Oakes.*

There are many explanations for the road's odd name, though no one seems to know for sure how it came about. Those who named it are no longer around, and so we are left to wonder. According to some, Shades of Death Road, a seven-mile stretch that skirts sod farms, woods and meadows in the Pequest River Valley alongside Jenny Jump Mountain, was first known by the bucolic moniker the Shades on account of its canopy of leafy green leaves. When bandits who lived in the nearby woods began to rob and kill passing travelers—prompting local residents to respond by catching and hanging said bandits from those same leafy trees—the pastoral name took an ominous turn. Others say the name came from a series of murders that occurred there, beginning with those same early bandits, who would kill not only passing travelers but one another as well, in their frequent fights over women. And when reports of brutal murders along the eerie road continued well into the twentieth century, its bloody reputation was solidified. Some have said the name refers to a massacre that occurred in the days of the Lenape and the many bodies of tribesmen that were buried there. The name might also connect to the legend of a little girl named Jenny, who jumped from the nearby mountain, now named in her honor, to save herself from capture, only to fall to her death.

Not all the death was said to have been dealt by human hands. According to some sources, early settlers and travelers along Shades of Death Road often fell victim to predatory wildcats that were believed to prowl the region. And others mention attacks by poisonous snakes, some even falling from the trees overhead.

Probably the most credible explanation for the road's ghastly name involves outbreaks of malaria that were said to have occurred here when swarms of mosquitoes would emerge each summer from the surrounding wetlands, resulting in many deaths. The annual bouts of sickness and death continued to torment local residents until, in the late nineteenth century, the state finally drained the wetlands, driving off the malarial insects but leaving behind the name that they inspired.

Its origin uncertain, the name "Shades of Death" remains today one of the many mysteries that emerge from the murky depths of history. And since no one seems to know for sure where it came from, we have some license to entertain possibilities, including, perhaps, some long-ago encounter with a roadside ghost. After all, not only does "death" have its obvious implications, but one meaning of "shade" is "ghost."

Whether or not early residents saw spirits along this road, many today have made claims, leading to an ever-growing body of lore and an increasingly spooky reputation. Some have called Shades of Death the scariest road in New Jersey; others go so far as to include it on lists of the scariest places on Earth. A quick online search yields an abundance of videos, some claiming to contain footage of authentic paranormal activity. Stories persist of hauntings, curses and disappearances, and many are drawn by these accounts to drive this dark and lonely stretch seeking contact with something unseen. Myself included.

It was late on a gray October afternoon when I threaded my way through the twists and turns of Southtown Road, close to where it connects with Shades of Death. Fresh from my hunt for the White Pilgrim, I hoped to have time to drive the haunted road before nightfall. And as the waxing moon rose above a close canopy of trees, still clutching their leaves, I raced toward Shades of Death.

Approaching the intersection, I thought about the stories I'd heard, including those shared by contributors to *Weird NJ*. One was the legend of a Native American spirit said to appear to drivers in the guise of a ghostly deer. He would charge an oncoming car, and if the driver failed to stop, they would later get into an accident. Another contributor claimed to have been followed closely along the road by a mysterious light that vanished as quickly as it came. And the reports of strange phenomena are not restricted to the road itself; drivers have claimed to see odd lights and spectral figures moving through the surrounding woods, some coming right up to the road's edge.

In *Spooky New Jersey*, author S.E. Schlosser mentions the ghost of a woman who reportedly beheaded her husband beside the road, as well as phantom footsteps in the mud or snow. But, as Schlosser writes, people are often so busy hunting for the most conspicuous sightings, they may miss the subtler spirits, such as the gossamer ghosts of the Lenape said to linger in wisps of fog.

So, as I pulled onto Shades of Death Road, I kept my eyes wide in the dimming light, hoping to catch a glimpse of those subtle spirits. But I had to wonder whether these reports were authentic, or were they only the creations of an active imagination inspired by evocative places with suggestive names? There on that lonely stretch of road surrounded by the darkening woods, I wasn't sure which I preferred.

Soon, I approached a small body of water on the side of the road known as Ghost Lake. And as I passed it, I noticed how the sky seemed brighter there, a phenomenon that others have noted and some believe to be supernatural. Peering through the trees on the far side, I saw an orb of pale light. *Only the moon*, I thought. But that was cold comfort as the sky grew darker and the shadows seemed to move.

Spirits are said to appear in the tendrils of fog that often swirl over Ghost Lake, many, though not all, identified as Lenape, even though this man-made lake did not exist in the days when their people inhabited the area. According to reports, the lake was created in the 1940s by two local landowners named Leon Hull and William Crouse Jr., who gave the lake its spooky name and dubbed other nearby landmarks "Haunted Hollow" and "Murderer's Mountain," in an apparent bid to scare off would-be trespassers.

Even though the name may not have been inspired by any actual ghost sighting, many claim to spot spirits on the lake today. In *Ghosthunting New Jersey*, L'Aura Hladik tells of an undead bride and groom said to have been seen emerging from the lake. And local resident Bob Parichuk told me about the wraithlike shapes in the fog that a friend of his once reported seeing.

After looking for ghosts over the lake that bears their name, I continued down Shades of Death Road, hoping to drive its length before night fell. And as I rounded the curves under low limbs and a violet sky, I peered into the darkness at the edge of my headlights, wondering what strange things

The sky seemed brighter over Ghost Lake, a phenomenon that some believe to be supernatural. *Robert Oakes.*

might appear just beyond the next bend. I could feel the wheels turning in my mind, the spirit of invention on a cold October night on a road called Shades of Death.

CLINTON ROAD

Growing up in Jersey, just like kids anywhere, we would get bored, and just like everybody everywhere, we would sometimes tell stories about scary local places just to give ourselves a thrill. For us, those stories were often set in the woods, because when you're from suburbia, the woods are where the scary is—in the darkness on the edge of town. Much of the thrill of those places was their wildness. Outside the circle of streetlights on the paved roads we knew so well was an unlit, unpaved world that was utterly unfamiliar and unknown. And with the unknown came the fear.

For me, it was enough to know that these places were out there, to visit them through the transportive power of a story. But those who wanted a more visceral thrill would get in the car and go, to investigate for themselves whether the stories were true and maybe become a part of one in the process.

Clinton Road in northwestern Passaic County was the perfect place to go—near enough to get to from suburbia but heavily forested and mostly undeveloped because it crossed land reserved for the Newark Watershed. It was an easily accessible ten-mile stretch of mysterious twists and turns through the dark and dangerous woods we loved to fear.

And it helped that the area had long been known for its spookiness. In 1873, local historian and itinerant schoolteacher Joseph Percy Crayon wrote this about the nearby woods: "In the days of the Revolution these woods were infested by bands of robbers and counterfeiters, and true believers in witches and ghosts asserted that their 'departed spirits' were more terrible to meet and numerous than wild animals." And that was many years ago. The Clinton Road legends, as reported in *Weird NJ* and many other print and online sources, have grown quite a lot since then. Indeed, the sheer volume and variety of paranormal reports associated with the area are truly dizzying.

Some of the lore is connected to certain roadside structures, such as a pyramidical stack of stones that some call the "Druid temple," which is actually what remains of the Clinton Furnace, used in the production of iron here between 1833 and 1852. Added to the National Register of Historic Places in 1976, the structure stands—off-limits to the public but visible from the road—as a testament to the robust iron industry that once existed throughout this part of Passaic County and lower New York State, though some insist it is a cursed place where secret nocturnal rites are performed.

Similar stories circulate around the ruins of what is known locally as Cross Castle. Built in 1907 by English-born New York City banker Richard J. Cross, Bearfort House, as Cross named it, was a massive stone estate that stood on 365 acres of woods, fields and farmland near a 77-acre body of water known as Hank's Pond. After Cross died in 1917, his family sold the property to the City of Newark, and for years it stood, silently overlooking Clinton Valley. However, after a fire made the walls structurally unsound and numerous incidents of vandalism and trespassing were reported, the Newark Watershed Commission tore down the remaining stone walls in 1988. Many locals still recall late-night gatherings at the site, and to this day, stories persist of satanic rituals among the ruins, as well as strange sounds, sensations, visions and apparitions.

But not all of the paranormal tales are attached to those structures; many emanate from all along this spooky stretch of road, which is also said to be frequented by mobsters and Ku Klux Klansmen. Some of the reports include sounds like disembodied voices, screams, the laughter of children or the sound of chanting. Some have reportedly seen shadow figures or odd individuals watching from the woods or standing in the road. There have been claims of orbs, fireballs and other strange lights in the sky or over the water. Electronic devices have been said to go haywire, and weather has been said to change drastically. And some have claimed to feel sick or lose time while driving along the road.

Strange creatures have also been reported: monkeys and mutant animals, as well as what some have described as hole-digging demons. And of course, it wouldn't be New Jersey without a Jersey Devil sighting or two. But probably the creature most associated with Clinton Road is what has been described as a wolf-like animal with glowing eyes, said to be fast enough to keep pace with passing cars and to tear off paint with its claws or fangs.

Plenty of other entities are said to haunt Clinton Road. Reports include ghosts in the castle and the old furnace, undead park rangers and a disembodied hand said to wander the woods on moonlit nights. The spirit of an old woman is said to walk beside cars, and a ghost boy armed with a stick has been said to chase people through the woods.

And as you can imagine, many of the Clinton Road stories involve cars. Some say that the spirits of those killed in car accidents haunt the area where they died, often at one particularly sharp turn known as Dead Man's Curve. And many have claimed to be chased down Clinton Road by a phantom vehicle, most often described as a black pickup truck. Those who report such incidents say these ghost truckers appear without warning—driving aggressively, flashing their lights—only to disappear suddenly.

But of all the many reports associated with Clinton Road, probably the best known and most iconic is the story of a ghost boy who haunts a bridge. There are various versions of this tale, but according to most, the boy was killed by a passing motorist while walking on a bridge along the road. Many say you can contact this spirit by throwing a coin from the bridge into the water below. Shortly thereafter, he will either throw the coin back to you or leave it on the road for you to find. Some have claimed to see the boy's face in the water or to see him standing on the bridge. Many locate this phenomenon at Dead Man's Curve; however, others say it occurs at the small stone bridge just up the road from the furnace. In either location, it isn't unusual to find a heap of coins in the water below, tossed there by many past hopefuls.

Those who make it through this gauntlet of ghosts must face one final fright, the scariest of all to a Jerseyan: what has been called the state's longest traffic light at the intersection of Clinton Road and Route 23.

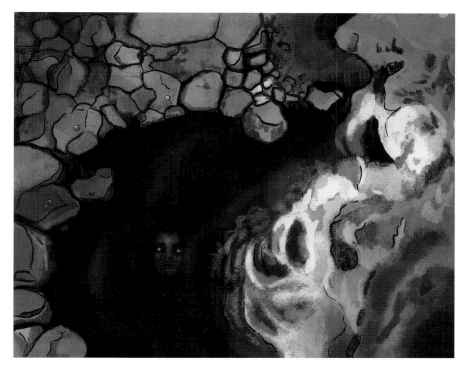

Many say you can contact the boy's spirit by throwing a coin from the bridge into the water below. *Katherine Oakes.*

Judging by reports of the many visitors who venture there, Clinton Road continues to have a powerful pull. As for me, I still think the best way to go there is through the tales we tell about it and let it remain a mysterious unknown in the darkness on the edge of town.

CHAPTER 11

IN AWE OF THE
PAULINSKILL VIADUCT

As I drove beneath the Paulinskill Viaduct near Knowlton Township and glanced up at its concrete arches among the leaves overhead, I felt something I can only describe as awe. And no wonder. When it was first built in the early 1900s to allow the Lackawanna Cutoff railway to cross the Paulins Kill, the viaduct, also known as the Hainesburg Trestle, was an architectural marvel, the largest reinforced concrete structure in existence at the time. Looking up at it today, even in its abandoned state, covered as it is with water stains and graffiti, it's easy to understand why it was regarded with such reverence, with its sturdy towers holding up seven impressive arches over the river and road below. And as the line between awe and fear is often very thin, it's also easy to understand why many have felt the presence of fearful things in and around this massive structure.

Built between 1908 and 1910 by the Delaware, Lackawanna & Western Railroad, the Paulinskill Viaduct, which measures 1,100 feet long and 115 feet tall, opened for rail traffic in 1911 and continued to operate until 1979. The line was abandoned in the early 1980s, at which time the tracks were removed. But recently, there has been talk of restoring passenger rail service along the Lackawanna Cutoff, which would likely include reopening the viaduct. It would mean the resurrection of this historically significant overpass, which has become the fascination of thrill-seeking urban adventurers and, if the stories are true, the haunt of restless spirits.

A ghost train has been seen crossing the overpass on especially dark and murky nights. *Katherine Oakes.*

Much of the lore that swirls around the Paulinskill Viaduct involves the spirit of one of the workmen who helped build it. Some say the man died after falling into unset concrete and that his body was never recovered. They say he is entombed inside the viaduct and his spirit now roams the trestle at night, particularly along the railway bed. Several people have reported a chilling presence there that they attributed to this workman's ghost, along with the feeling of being watched.

According to another account, a ghost train has been seen crossing the overpass on especially dark and murky nights. Others claim that the hollow chambers in the bridge's concrete structure are often used as a place to summon evil spirits during satanic rituals, pointing to the many cryptic symbols and messages on the walls as evidence of this activity.

Despite these eerie reports, thrill-seekers continue to be drawn to the viaduct. Even though it is off-limits to the public, many have reportedly climbed to the top to take in the view or to explore the chambers under the railway bed. And according to reports, some have ridden ATVs across the bridge or have even dared to bungee from it.

As impressive as it is, I didn't want to linger anywhere near that concrete span. Something about it made me feel uneasy. And given the recent complaints by local residents about trespassing, as well as the warnings and arrests by the state police, I decided it was best to keep moving. I certainly had no desire to climb up there. It's dangerous and illegal, and it's understandable why such activity is discouraged. But it was more than the illegality of it that made me want to move along. Maybe it was the way it towered over me that gave me that awe of massive things. Or maybe it was that same fearful feeling in the air that so many have attributed to the spirits of the Paulinskill Viaduct.

CHAPTER 12
THE LEGEND OF
THE FLANDERS HOOKERMAN

How do ghost legends come to be? Some may be inspired by an authentic occult experience, while others are born of pure imagination. And still others may arise from phenomena that only seem paranormal if you don't know the natural forces at work behind them. Fancy kicks in to fill the gaps in understanding, and *voila*! A ghost is born. This may explain how the legend of the Flanders Hookerman came to be.

For decades, local residents spoke of an unusual orb of light near the Flanders section of Mount Olive Township in Morris County. Many claimed to see the orb along the Jersey Central Railroad's High Bridge Branch where it once skirted the South Branch of the Raritan River near North Four Bridges and Bartley Roads. Others said it drifted nearer to Naughright Road in Washington Township, Budd Lake or even as far south as Hillsborough in Somerset County or as far north as Boonton. The mysterious light was said to appear above the tracks at dusk or late at night, sometimes orange in color, sometimes yellow, green, red or white. It would manifest suddenly, then vanish and reappear, moving closer and closer, bobbing side to side. Some said it resembled a flashlight or a lantern. Some said they could see standing behind it a translucent figure in overalls holding up the light with one raised hand—his only hand. All that was left of the other was a hook.

This, they said, was the Hookerman, a nineteenth-century railroad worker who lost his lower arm to the steel wheels after falling from a car onto the tracks. For years after this incident, the man was said to walk there with a lantern hanging from the hook he'd been given as a prosthesis, searching in

Some said they could see, standing behind the orb, a translucent figure with a hook for a hand. *Katherine Oakes.*

vain all the rest of his days for the limb he lost and the wedding band still attached to it. And now, they said, if you see that orb approaching, it's the Hookerman still searching in the afterlife. And anyone who gets in the way of his ghost may feel the sharp end of his hook.

Despite such eerie reports and grim warnings, searching for the Hookerman became a popular pastime, especially among local teenagers. Many recall Friday night frights, driving past a railroad crossing with a carful of friends hoping to catch a glimpse. Some would even get out to investigate, only to turn and run when the Hookerman light would appear.

And according to the reports, the orb did indeed appear—many times to many people. In fact, sightings became so frequent and widespread that various experts began to study the phenomenon to try to determine its cause. According to *Weird NJ*, in 1976 a group known as Vestigia did manage to capture evidence of the phenomenon, including an actual photograph of the orb. A number of theories have since been put forward to explain it, including the combustion of natural gasses, ball lightning and a phenomenon known as triboluminescence, by which intense pressure produces flashes of light.

Because the railway lay over quartz-laden stone along a fault line known as the Ramapo Border Fault, the theory is, occasional minor earthquakes may provide the stress needed to produce the triboluminescent effect, resulting in a momentary orb of light that would drift slowly for some distance, conducted by the steel rails. And indeed, it seems as though people stopped seeing the lights once the rails were removed in the late 1970s.

The Flanders light is actually one of many similar phenomena—referred to as ghost lights or spook lights—that have been observed in various locations throughout the United States. These include the Marfa Lights in Texas and the Tri-State Spook Light at the intersection of Kansas, Oklahoma and Missouri. And just like in New Jersey, these phenomena have inspired both scientific theories and ghostly legends. Among the ones that most closely resemble Jersey's ghost light are the Maco Light in North Carolina, the Gurdon Light in Arkansas and the Paulding Light in Michigan. Just like in Jersey, these lights were seen along old railroad tracks. And just like in Jersey, they were said to be the lantern of a brakeman who died in a railway accident.

Ghost lights and the stories they inspire have actually been with us for centuries, appearing in the lore of many world cultures. Probably the best-known ghost light in European folklore is the will-o'-the-wisp. Often seen over swamps or bogs, these lights were said to mislead lost travelers who believed them to be the lanterns of helpful guides, though they were actually ghosts, fairies or other elemental spirits abroad in the night visiting mischief upon the unwary. Or so the old stories would have you believe. Today, scientists theorize that these lights are caused by the combustion of flammable gasses naturally found in bogs, by noncombustion chemical reactions or by bioluminescence.

Still, the stories remain. In fact, the Flanders Hookerman isn't the only ghost light legend to be found in this part of the state. Indeed, it seems New Jersey may have its own resident will-o'-the-wisp. In *The Roads of Home*, Henry Charlton Beck describes his conversation with a retired Jersey Central station agent named Bill Banghart from Glen Gardner. Bill told Beck of "a man named Fritz who had met his death after a 'battle' with a will-o'-the-wisp." Bill said the incident took place near Woodglen in present-day Lebanon Township:

> *That was where* [Fritz] *said he saw a ball of fire rise out of the ground near the woods. He swore at it a little and then threw a stone to hit it. Next morning, he was dead. Don't know what there was to the story, but I remember that the youngsters around here never wanted to go by the place.*

And not all of the railroad ghosts in the area are said to be that of the Hookerman. In *Tales and Towns of Northern New Jersey*, Beck also mentions the legend of a disembodied head seen floating over the tracks of the Morris & Essex Railroad. Such an abundance of stories about railroad ghosts with missing limbs or disembodied heads says much about the very real fears and dangers faced by those who worked the rails. And indeed, quite a few accidents, injuries and deaths occurred while these railway lines were in operation.

Because thrill-seekers on the hunt for the Hookerman's ghost also faced real dangers even after the High Bridge line was abandoned, the rails were removed in the 1970s, and eventually, the property became part of the Columbia Trail, a fifteen-mile recreational path that runs through both Morris and Hunterdon Counties. Thousands today experience it as a peaceful and pastoral place for biking, hiking, snowshoeing and cross-country skiing. And reports of orbs have dwindled down to none. But many here remember the moment when they first saw the light. And for them, that eerie memory and the Hookerman's sad tale still linger like a phantom train along this ghost of a railway line.

CHAPTER 13
TALES FROM THE HAUNTED FOREST

DREW UNIVERSITY

Drew University in Madison holds a special place in my heart. One of my childhood friends was a student there, and I used to visit him on campus. I also dated someone who went there, and as a singer/ songwriter, I played frequently in the campus coffeehouse, the Other End. I never took a single class at Drew, but for a little while, at least, I could often be found haunting the place. So it warmed me to find that the school so heartily celebrates its ghosts. Indeed, Drew University gives an entirely new meaning to school spirit.

Founded in 1867 as a Methodist seminary, Drew has grown over the last century and a half to become a top liberal arts college with undergraduate and graduate programs and a school of theology. Because Drew is known as the "University in the Forest," on account of its 186 beautifully wooded acres, and also happens to be known as one of the most haunted colleges in America, "Tales from the Haunted Forest" is a very fitting title for the ghost tours and presentations now offered there by university archivist and assistant librarian Matthew Beland.

From my very first email inquiry, it was clear to me that Matthew was the man to see for all things ghosts at Drew. He replied with a whole host of documents, images, reports and podcasts from the archive, along with links to a website and videos he and his colleagues had produced—all in celebration of the institution's haunted reputation. And he generously agreed to meet with me on campus to show me some of the paranormal hot spots.

Mead Hall, photographed here in 1885, is a focus of Drew's paranormal lore. *Drew University Archives.*

I arrived on a bright and blustery morning, my mind filled with ghosts of my own—memories of moments I had spent there years ago and of the people I once knew, brief flashes of personal history against the backdrop of buildings that seemed mostly unchanged. Matthew met me beside the impressive stone columns of historic Mead Hall and led me into this grand Greek Revival mansion that now serves as the main administrative hub of the school—and as a focus of its paranormal lore.

This palatial brick, brownstone and marble house was built in 1836 by wealthy Savannah plantation owner William Gibbons on a substantial parcel of land—known even then as "the Forest"—where Gibbons could pursue his passion for Thoroughbred horse racing. When Gibbons died in 1852, his son William took up ownership, but after supporting the Confederates during the Civil War, the younger Gibbons was forced to sell the property in 1867 to New York City financier Daniel Drew. A devout Methodist, Drew donated the property to the church to house a theological seminary, which they named in his honor. The mansion was rechristened Mead Hall after Drew's wife, Roxanna Mead.

"Mead Hall is, arguably, the most famous building on campus," Matthew told me as we stepped into the entrance hall. And it's one of the most famously haunted. My gaze immediately fell on the painting of a stern-faced woman on the far wall beside the main stairs.

"That's Roxanna Mead," Matthew said. "People say she haunts that painting." And I can understand why. Her penetrating eyes seemed to follow us as we moved across the hall.

Indeed, many have reported a presence in and around the painting. According to the Drew website, Roxanna's portrait gave one student such a creepy feeling that she simply couldn't look at it. And L'Aura Hladik, in *Ghosthunting New Jersey*, reported that a school administrator once claimed to see a bright light leave the painting, float across the hall to a mirror, move to another mirror and then return to the painting.

Matthew pointed out that Roxanna Mead never actually lived in this house and that members of the Gibbons family and household staff, some of whom did die here, were more likely to haunt it. Still, the stories of Roxanna's ghost persist. Some say she appears as a lady in white descending the stairs or walking the halls. Others, including security officers and maintenance staff, have reported the sound of footsteps and opening doors, often late at night when they know the building to be empty. There have also been temperature fluctuations, electrical anomalies, eerie sensations and the appearance of orbs—all attributed to the ghost of Roxanna Mead.

Down in the basement, Matthew showed me the area that had been used as living quarters for the Gibbons's formerly enslaved African American servants and wondered aloud whether any of their spirits might haunt the house. He also shared with me a story from one of his colleagues, who said she once felt the touch of an unseen hand while standing in the basement. And according to the Drew website, a security officer and a night maintenance person once reported seeing a hazy mass, about four feet from the floor, move silently around the corner of a wall, then recoil quickly as if surprised to find the men there. This happened, they said, several times before the form vanished entirely. The two men then searched the entire building but found nothing.

Probably the most impressive report at Mead Hall involves the massive fire, in August 1989, that caused severe damage to the building. While fighting the blaze, two firemen said they saw a woman dressed in period clothing walking toward them from the burning building. As they ran to help her, she vanished. Apparently, a photographer on site captured an image of this woman, though I have not seen it. But people say it was the

Many have reported Roxanna Mead's ghost near her painting in the hall that bears her name. Some say they have seen her descending the stairs. *Robert Oakes.*

ghost of Roxanna Mead emerging from the house that night, untouched by the fire that threatened her namesake. Indeed, the spirit of Mead Hall was undiminished by this catastrophe; like a phoenix, it rose again, completely rebuilt and restored within only a few years.

Matthew led me next to Seminary Hall. Built in 1899 as an administrative building, this hall now houses the theological school. It's in the Craig Chapel on the second floor where most of the paranormal activity is said to occur.

"People have claimed to hear the pipe organ play on its own," Matthew said, as he pointed to a set of metal pipes in the corner of the room. "Now, if the pipes were left open, wind from an open window could blow through them and make a sound. But one security officer who heard it said, 'No, I didn't hear a sound like wind running through the pipes. I heard church music. I heard a tune being played.'"

Matthew also relayed the story of a maintenance worker who, while cleaning the chapel in the dead of winter, said he felt the room turn suddenly cold and saw shadows cast by the pews begin to move, though the overhead chandeliers were still. He said he turned off the lights and left the room, only to find them on again when he returned. This happened three times, he reported.

A contributor to *Weird NJ* said he heard heavy breathing one evening while praying in the chapel and said the sound was accompanied by an unseen presence and the feeling of being watched. And one commenter on social media alluded to a much more intrusive entity in the chapel, calling it a "wailing ghost."

The next building we visited was made of brown brick with carved letters on the facade proclaiming "Bowne Gymnasium," though Matthew explained that this building was no longer dedicated to athletics as it had been when it was constructed in 1909. Today, it is the home of the F.M. Kirby Shakespeare Theater and, if the legends are true, also home to one of the few named ghosts on campus, Reggie, who reportedly drowned in the pool once housed inside. Known to be a mischievous puller of pranks, Reggie is said to cause stage accidents and lighting malfunctions, to move furniture and to make props go missing. He has been seen walking up a spiral staircase wearing a vintage running suit or changing his clothes in the area where the men's locker room once was. Like thespians everywhere, the theater professionals who work here tend to be superstitious and take no chances when it comes to Reggie. Every time they leave, they wish him a good night, believing it will bring luck, or at least keep the prankster ghost appeased.

Our next stop, S.W. Bowne Hall, loomed above us like a castle in a dark medieval landscape. The Great Hall on the second floor, with its wood paneling, carved beams, large fireplace and leaded glass windows, was modeled after the hall at Oxford's Christ Church College. It's so Hogwartsian, I fully expected an appearance from Nearly Headless Nick. But no, the ghost of the Great Hall is said to be a man in gold glasses who makes the chandeliers sway even when the air is still. Or, if he's feeling frisky, he might push people toward the door as if asking them to leave. Other reports in this room include the sound of phantom piano and the appearance of faces in the ceiling beams.

We continued on to probably the most haunted building on campus—even more haunted than Mead Hall—the dorm known to students as Hoyt. Built in 1894, Hoyt-Bowne Hall, as it's formally known, is the oldest of the student residences, and as such, it has had the most time to inspire tales. Most of the reports are centered on the infamous fourth floor, which many believe to be haunted by a misandrist female spirit, though the cause of her hatred for men varies from story to story. Some say she was raped and then

The Bowne Gymnasium, photographed here in the early 1900s, is said to be haunted by a ghost named Reggie. *Drew University Archives.*

killed herself, others say she hanged herself after she was abandoned by the man who got her pregnant and still others say she was thrown from a fourth-floor window by a male attacker. Whatever the reason, it is believed that any man who goes up onto the fourth floor becomes her victim. Men have reportedly been scratched and knocked down, have suffered broken limbs and have been made to feel exceedingly uneasy. Some students have named this spirit Carol and have even claimed to see her, describing her long dark hair. According to the Drew website, five students once claimed to see the dark-haired woman in an attic window, silhouetted against a bright light inside the room. The group circled the building to inspect the other windows, and on returning to the front, they discovered that a shade had been pulled down in front of the window. They then entered the building and climbed to the attic, only to find it completely dark.

Many students have also reported odd sounds emanating from the fourth floor, including footsteps, creaking, music and objects falling. But the odd phenomena are not limited to that floor. All over the building, students have reported doors and windows opening and closing on their own, shades flying

S.W. Bowne Hall looms above the campus like a castle in a dark medieval landscape. *Robert Oakes.*

up, knocks and nudges by an unseen hand, digital clocks changing time, TVs turning on, lights flickering, the appearance of a glowing red orb of light and socks and other objects going missing—all attributed to Carol or perhaps some other resident ghost.

Even outside the building, spirits are said to prowl. Students have claimed to see the phantom of a Revolutionary War–era soldier that seemed to pop up from the ground and then vanish suddenly. Such reports have given rise to the belief that Hoyt-Bowne Hall was built on top of a colonial cemetery.

Matthew brought me to the back of the building and showed me the second-story window of what had been the dorm of a young man named George Lose back in 1902. While digging through the archives, Matthew learned that this unfortunate seminary student was electrocuted in that room when he placed his feet on a radiator while reaching for a reading lamp and unwittingly completed the circuit of an electrical surge that had passed through the building's heating pipes. Matthew wondered whether any of the hauntings could be caused by the ghost of young Mr. Lose, still haunting the building where he suffered such a sudden and shocking death.

Haunted Hoyt-Bowne Hall circa 1918. *Drew University Archives.*

The final stop on our tour that morning was Asbury Hall. Originally built in the 1830s as a stable for Gibbons's horses, it serves today as another residential hall, where it is believed a seminary student once hanged himself from the attic rafters. Many say his spirit haunts the hallways and stairwells, manifesting as a mist, a shadow, cold spots, strange noises or an unseen presence.

There are many more reportedly active locations on the Drew campus than we had time to explore that day. One such place is the Zuck Arboretum, a wild area that serves as a peaceful retreat for students and a sanctuary for plants, trees, turtles, geese and other wildlife, as well as, perhaps, something more supernatural. Stories have spread throughout the campus community of a lady in blue that hovers over one of the arboretum's glacial ponds. Apparently, no one has yet seen her face, only her long blue dress. But she is said to appear most often at sunset, and in one of the stories, she offered a stone of protection to the student who encountered her. Reports have also come in from the archival vaults, the library and the coffeehouse, as well as several other residential halls. Judging by the sheer number of stories, Drew certainly lives up to its haunted reputation.

As we walked back toward Mead Hall, I asked Matthew whether he believes in ghosts and whether he's ever experienced one himself. He said

The lights of S.W. Bowne Hall are reflected in Tipple Pond in this photograph from the mid-1900s. *Drew University Archives.*

that while he has been to the eeriest places on campus, he has yet to witness anything strange. And so he remains a skeptic. However, he said, a number of his friends and colleagues have reported unusual things, and he "would never gainsay anyone else's beliefs and experiences." Rather, he celebrates the mystery of it all and loves to share the lore.

In one of the podcasts he sent me, *Once Upon a Time: A Storytelling Podcast,* hosted by Talia Smith, Matthew explained how the school came to embrace its paranormal history and how Matthew was tapped to be its ghost ambassador. "In 2016, the library was looking for ways to reach out to undergraduate students," he said. During a brainstorming session, the head of the library asked, "'What's something that's catchy? Ghosts! We have this ghost heritage. Why don't we do a thing on Halloween?'"

Asked to lead this new initiative, Matthew created a presentation based on documents and images he had pulled from the archive, which he then delivered to a student audience in the guise of an undead professor. And just like that, a new school tradition was born. Even through the COVID lockdown of 2020, when classes were held remotely, Matthew and his team continued to share the presentations and tours online and even live-streamed through the night from some of the most haunted places on campus, an idea dreamed up by Matthew's colleague Candace Reilly.

"We just kept on running with it because it was super popular," Matthew observed. It certainly helps that ghosts are popular, but Matthew believes this lore also serves a very meaningful purpose. It offers "a way to help people connect to this place that they live in and connect to a rich history…that we just naturally forget.…You come into a dorm room, and you think…that's your room." But others were here before us, other lives were lived here, "and that's a connection I was eager to form.…It really does reshape your experience with a place, and I think it helps us connect to this mysterious past that is still present with us through these buildings."

Matthew believes that these ghost stories also encourage a sense of school unity and pride.

> Stories build community. And I think this helps give something special to Drew students, to the Drew community, that they can then share.….And my job as the archivist is…to give historical evidence that dovetails or connects with the stories and makes them come alive. And it's been great. I'm so grateful to my superiors here who thought, Let's do ghosts! Because it's been undergraduate outreach gold. It's worked perfectly, and it continues to serve us and help us in so many ways. And it helps me share the history of this institution, which I love so much.

Apart from my own memories of the past, I didn't see any ghosts at Drew that day. But I left "the Forest" feeling I had found a kindred spirit in Matthew. I was so happy to have met him, to see how he and the school celebrate their ghost lore and to visit that beautiful campus one more time. While Drew isn't my alma mater, I felt school spirit for it all the same.

CHAPTER 14

IN SEARCH OF
MORRISTOWN'S GHOSTS

HAUNTED HISTORY

By the time Morristown became the nerve center of the American Revolution in the late 1770s, it had, for decades, been the commercial and political hub of Morris County. For those who worked the iron mines, forges and furnaces throughout the surrounding countryside, Morristown offered a place to conduct business and purchase supplies. Its square, known as the Green, lay at the heart of the town, overseeing militia musters, court trials and executions and providing pastureland and a place for public gatherings.

As the Revolutionary War raged, Washington and his men found winter refuge in Morristown, protected from the British by the surrounding Watchung Mountains and Great Swamp. But that protection came at a cost. During the winter of 1779–80, Washington's men endured disease, hunger and extreme cold as they camped at nearby Jockey Hollow, cramped into small vermin-infested huts, many without pay, some without adequate clothing. The frequent death of their comrades became a simple fact of life. According to *Historical Collections of the State of New Jersey* by Barber and Howe:

> *When the sickness was at its height, no less than 40 coffins were brought at one time, and piled against the barn…callous and inured to the horrors that beset them, the soldiers, regardless of all, were seen playing cards upon coffins containing the remains of their deceased comrades.*

The local community also suffered during this time as hungry soldiers raided food supplies, and frequent false alarms warning of imminent British attacks sent tremors through the town.

As bitter as wartime was, Morristown and the rest of the county became prosperous in the years that followed. Turnpikes and railroads brought access for residents and industry. The ironworks boomed, and wealthy New Yorkers built luxurious mansions, drawing in with them a sizable workforce. At the close of the Gilded Age, though, many of those wealthy estate owners departed, and a number of the mansions were torn down. But the overall population continued to grow and diversify, helped by the construction of new housing developments, interstates and highways. Today's Morristown is a bustling, modern town but one that retains a strong sense of its past. Many sites where significant American history was made are maintained and available to the public, including Morristown National Historical Park, dedicated in 1933. There visitors can explore several places where Washington and his men endured the "hard winter" of 1779.

In a town so suffused with history, it's perfectly conceivable that a spirit or two may linger. And indeed, stories have been told about ghost sightings and haunted locations in and around Morristown.

In *Spooky New Jersey*, S.E. Schlosser tells the story of a little girl ghost that saved George Washington from capture by the British one snowy night on the road from Summit to Morristown. And in the *Big Book of New Jersey Ghost Stories*, Martinelli and Stansfield write of the ghost of a little girl in the basement of a Victorian-style Morristown home. Could this be the same child spirit, still lingering through all the change and development wrought by the passing of centuries?

The authors do not identify this haunted Victorian home, but some of the Morristown mansions that are said to have resident ghosts are well known. Ford Mansion—where Washington and his wife, Martha, along with servants, guards and officers, waited out the brutal winter of 1779—is believed to be haunted by a number of entities. According to a 2016 article by Brian LaMuraglia on MorristownGreen.com, author and paranormal investigator Gordon Thomas Ward, who has led paranormal investigations and presentations at the mansion, said he once captured there the voice of what he supposed was the ghost of a female kitchen servant. And park ranger Joni Rowe, also quoted in the article, said she sometimes feels an unseen presence in the house.

The number of paranormal investigations that have recently been offered at historic sites throughout Morristown suggests a growing interest in local ghosts and perhaps an uptick in activity. Within the last several years, investigative groups have led ghost hunts at Fosterfields Living Historical Farm, the Frelinghuysen Mansion and the Vail House at Historic Speedwell, which has also played host to Halloween storytellers spinning spooky yarns.

While I found no mention of recent paranormal investigations at nearby Acorn Hall, activity at that nineteenth-century Italianate mansion was reported in several publications. In *Haunted Houses of New Jersey*, author Lynda Lee Macken identified the resident spirit as Louise Schermerhorn, who, along with her husband, Dr. John Schermerhorn, built the house in 1853. Tragically, Louise died shortly after the couple moved in, prompting her grief-stricken husband to sell the property in 1857 to Augustus and Mary Elizabeth Crane, whose family lived there until 1971 when it became a house museum and home of the Morris County Historical Society. According to Macken, the ghost of Louise has been seen descending the staircase, basket in hand, wearing a gown and bonnet, accompanied by the sound of footsteps and the soft rustle of fabric. L'Aura Hladik, in *Ghosthunting New Jersey*, also mentioned that psychics who have visited the home have felt the presence of a spirit in the area used as a gift shop.

THE SKIN OF ANTOINE LEBLANC

Among all these paranormal reports and eerie rumors, few have come to be as closely associated with Morristown as the story of Antoine LeBlanc, whose self-confessed crimes and grisly execution have left a lasting impression on the community. It's said by some that LeBlanc's ghost still walks in Morristown, mutilated and dissected. To understand how it came to be so dismembered, it will help to hear the entire gruesome tale.

Just after dawn on Sunday, May 12, 1833, a passerby discovered something unusual outside the home of prominent Morristonians Mr. and Mrs. Samuel Sayre: a bundle of Mr. Sayre's clothing. Receiving no answer when he knocked at the door, the man forced his way inside and gasped at what he found. The Sayre servant, Phoebe, lay dead, her head split with a hatchet. And outside in the barn, the Sayres themselves lay bludgeoned to death beneath a pile of manure. Their recently hired French laborer, Antoine LeBlanc, was nowhere to be found. With as many of the Sayres' valuables as he could stuff into a pillowcase, riding a horse he had taken from the stable,

LeBlanc was well on his way to New York City, where he hoped to set sail on the next available ship back home overseas.

What LeBlanc didn't know was that some of the stolen items had fallen from the back of his horse, leaving a trail that led the sheriff's posse right to where he had stopped to rest at a tavern in the meadows near Jersey City. After a brief struggle, the posse dragged the fugitive back to Morristown, where he confessed to the murders and was sentenced to hang.

Thousands of spectators descended on the Morristown Green to witness the execution. And once the twitching ceased and they were sure LeBlanc was dead, the body was cut down and sent to Dr. Isaac Canfield for dissection and study. Canfield, along with a group of physicians, then proceeded to perform experiments on the body, which included the use of electrical currents to attempt reanimation. They were able to produce a grin on his face, make his eyes roll and cause a few muscles to contract. But unlike Frankenstein's monster, Antoine LeBlanc stayed dead. Their experiments complete, the doctors then sent the body to the local tannery, where the skin was removed and used to make purses, wallets and other objects to sell as grisly souvenirs. It's said that, to this day, many of these objects may be found in and around Morristown, as well as in the archives of the New Jersey Historical Society in Newark.

The Sayre house, where the brutal murders had occurred, passed through several occupants until, in the late 1940s, it became the Winchester's Turnpike Inn, followed by establishments like the Wedgewood Inn, the Society Hill Restaurant and Jimmy's Haunt, before being torn down in 2007. During those years, customers, owners and staff alike told tales of strange experiences and unusual phenomena, all believed to be linked to that one awful night back in 1833. Reports included doors opening on their own, chandeliers moving, chairs rocking, candles lighting themselves, lights switching on in the middle of the night, whispers, loud voices, orbs and cold spots. One room in particular, believed to have been where Phoebe was murdered in her sleep, was often said to be exceedingly cold. Some reported seeing what appeared to be a hazy female form reflected in a mirror that hung there, and a waitress once reported the sensation of hands coming to rest on her shoulders as she walked through. One former owner claimed to witness the inexplicable explosion of a punch bowl, and another said his keys once suddenly went missing while he was alone in the building, only to reappear on his desk as his back was turned.

As for the identity of the spirit, it seems there was some disagreement. While many believed it to be the ghost of Phoebe, others felt sure it was

GHOSTS OF NORTHWESTERN NEW JERSEY

LeBlanc. Psychic mediums, including Ed and Lorraine Warren, were brought in to try to determine the identity and to help set the spirit free. According to *The Ghostly Register* by Arthur Myers, the Warrens believed it was LeBlanc. Myers also reported that they recommended a priest be brought in to perform an exorcism, which was done, successfully releasing the unhappy entity, they believed.

Even if LeBlanc's attachment to the Sayre house was severed, it may be that he still haunts the town. Indeed, some say he lingers there, seeking to restore the scattered pieces of his skin before his restless ghost can be at peace.

This story may be strongly associated with Morristown, but if the spirit of Antoine LeBlanc wants to be recognized as *the* Morristown Ghost, I'm afraid it has some competition. That title has already been given to two different entities, one in colonial times and the other in the late nineteenth century.

THE NINETEENTH-CENTURY MORRISTOWN GHOST

In 1886, several newspapers reported on a series of strange sightings throughout the town, beginning in the summer of 1885 with what seemed, at first, to be a tragic railway accident. According to an article in the *Democrat and Chronicle* out of Rochester, New York, a night train engineer said he thought he saw a man standing on the tracks, then heard the sound of bones crunching as the train appeared to mow him down. However, when the engineer got out to inspect the scene, he found no body beneath the wheels. Not long after this incident, others began to report a wandering spirit near the railway tracks, causing some to believe that what the engineer had seen that night was what the article called the Morristown Ghost.

That same year, the specter was also said to have lunged at a local physician as he rode home one night in his horse-drawn carriage. However, according to the report, this attack seemed not to have had the intended effect, as the doctor immediately "jumped from his carriage and caught the apparition." What happened next was left untold, but apparently the spirit got loose, because early the following year, the attacks began again, and this time, the ghost was not scared off so easily.

Its first victims were two men who had arrived in town by the midnight train. According to the article, the ghost "rose up tall and black and gaunt in front of the two men, waving his black hands at them…and thrust his hideous white face almost against their noses." Both men ran screaming from the scene as the phantom vanished in the night. When the apparition appeared again, it was to another man on another night near the same railroad station. The article reads: "It was tall and black and walked swiftly and noiselessly in the air....It passed on a short distance, then crossed the railroad, floated over the fence into a field, and vanished." This man simply froze in fear, watching it float out of sight. But another man who spotted the ghost "on a dark and lonely cross street" in West Morristown "was frightened into a moderately severe spasm."

After successfully terrifying the men of Morristown, the ghost then tried its charms on the women. But again, the tables were turned, because according to the report, the Morristown Ghost became more frightened of the women than they ever were of it. When accosted outside the Baptist cemetery, one woman "turned on the specter and cried out defiantly: 'Scare who? Scare who? Who will you scare?'" The ghost, apparently frightened by this unexpected challenge, "promptly vanished in the direction of the horse-shed." Another woman was similarly unimpressed when it appeared "waving his black hands at her...his ghostly white face...bent down close in

The women were unimpressed by the Morristown Ghost. *Katherine Oakes.*

front of hers." According to the article, this woman "looked calmly at the hideous visage, and…said in a quiet tone of conviction: 'O, it's you, is it?'"

The women of Morristown, in fact, were so angered by these attacks that, when it was announced that the ghost had been captured, they demanded a chance to take their revenge. As it turned out, the reports were false; the spirit was still at large, and so the women were denied their chance to lash it with whips, as they were prepared to do.

Whether this Morristown Ghost was ever apprehended, the article doesn't say. Nor was it determined whether it was truly an undead entity, though the discovery in a nearby barn of a white mask and black gloves and cloak certainly suggests a living prankster in a ghostly disguise.

THE ORIGINAL MORRISTOWN GHOST

From a prankster, we turn now to a huckster, Ransford Rogers, who, it may be said, was the *original* Morristown Ghost.

In the early part of the nineteenth century, multitudes were drawn to a place called Schooley's Mountain—about twenty miles west of Morristown—to enjoy the beneficial effects of its famous mineral springs. But about twenty years prior, the draw to the mountain ridge was all about gold. Somewhere up in those heights, it was said, a treasure had been hidden by pirates or Tories, and if you could find it, it was yours for the taking—with only one little catch. You see, the mountain's gold was guarded by ghosts.

Such stories were widespread in those days, and like many early Americans, plenty of Morristonians believed not only that the treasure was up there but also that it was possible to acquire. They needed only to find someone who could guide them to the gold and dispel the spirits that guarded it. The man they found was Ransford Rogers, an itinerant schoolteacher from Connecticut with a knack for chemistry and a certain charismatic charm. Presenting himself as an expert in the dark arts, Rogers assured the treasure seekers that he could help them, but only if they did exactly as he said.

According to an article by Joseph F. Tuttle published in the *Historical Magazine* in 1872, which itself draws heavily from a pamphlet published in 1792, Rogers's first task was to win the trust of the community, to make them believe that he could raise the ghosts. So he invited eight men to a kind of religious service at one of the local homes. After leading a prayer, he spoke solemnly of the fearful work before them. Somewhere up on that mountain was gold enough for everyone, but the guardian spirits were fierce, and they must be appeased. First, though, they must be raised. Then Rogers made a sudden movement, and immediately there came a thumping on the roof and walls, and a spectral voice said, "Press forward." Any man who was not convinced by this spectacle was certainly won over when, several nights later, someone reported seeing what appeared to be a white-sheeted figure gliding over the town.

Word spread, and soon upward of fifty treasure seekers were attending secret meetings at which Rogers led the men in prayer, admonished them to live righteously and promised them rich rewards. A potent liquor called applejack was often served, and at some point in the evening, a spirit would appear outside the house with its raps and its thumps and its encouraging edict: "Press forward."

Then the night came at last when the men were to meet the whole company of spirits face to face. The appointed place was a field up on the mountain ridge, close to the edge of the woods. A severe storm bent the branches and lit the night with lightning as they traveled to the gathering ground. The men were told to stand inside circles that Rogers had drawn in the dirt, and whatever happened, he said, they must not step outside the line.

Then they felt the presence of something unseen in the woods, just beyond the illumination of their lanterns. A sudden explosion split the night—not a bolt of lightning but something much closer to the ground. And in the glare of red fire that rose from the blast, ghastly forms appeared, hideously groaning, faces hidden. Rogers, who had been leading the ritual, communed with the spirits, from whom he learned that if the men wanted their gold, they must each leave an offering of twelve pounds in hard coin underneath a tree. The men fell to their knees as Rogers continued his incantations and gesticulations deep into the night, until everything went quiet and they made their way back home, in awe of Ransford Rogers and in haste to pay the ghosts.

Through the coming winter, the men did all they could to raise the funds. Farms were mortgaged; horses and cattle were sold. The secret meetings continued, and each time, the spirits would appear outside the house, rapping on windows, jingling coins and encouraging the men to "press forward" and, above all, keep the whole business a secret. Any man who needed a little extra encouragement would receive his own private haunt outside his bedroom window from the same white-sheeted figure that had been seen gliding above the town.

As Rogers led the ritual in the glare of red fire, ghastly forms appeared, hideously groaning. *Katherine Oakes.*

Then the moment came when the men were to deliver their payment in exchange for the hidden treasure. Again they gathered in the glade, and again the spirits appeared in the woods all around them. And one by one, the men knelt by the appointed tree. With eyes averted, they left their offering—

as much coin as each man had been able to muster—and then looked up to find the money gone, apparently taken by the ghosts. But what came next surprised them all. Instead of leading the men to the treasure, the spirits scolded them. Some of the men had not kept the secret, they said. Some of them were faithless and immoral. The ghosts began to rage at the frightened gathering, and it was all Rogers could do to hold the angry spirits at bay. Finally, he was able to calm them down, and the men returned to town, heavy-hearted and defeated. What would they do now? How would they ever get their hands on the hidden gold of Schooley's Mountain?

Rogers, of course, had the answer: more secret meetings attended by even more congregants with more applejack and more mysterious rapping on the rooftops, walls and windows…and, naturally, more payments in hard coin. Only this would appease the spirits and move them to reveal the hidden gold.

During this time, rumors began to circulate. That same white-sheeted ghost was seen by many in Morristown. Someone said they saw it gliding from the rooftop of the courthouse to the tavern next door. A young woman milking a cow after dark said she saw it on the ridge of the barn, at which she dropped her pail and rain screaming into the house. Fear and superstition rose to a fever pitch. The spirits were all around them. Soon they would deliver to the secret congregants the treasure for which they had so fervently prayed—and paid. But only if they could keep the faith a little while longer.

So the secret meetings continued. And Rogers introduced new ways to commune with the dead—spirit writing and ritual movement—but always, the most effective way to keep the channel open was to keep the money—and the liquor—flowing. The white-sheeted figure would sometimes make an appearance outside the home of a worthy gentleman, inviting him to join their congregation—and to bring his purse, of course.

Another trip to the spirit meadow soon followed, and the congregants left another deposit beneath the tree. This time, each man was given in return a small envelope filled with dust said to be made from the buried bodies of the guardian ghosts. It was meant to serve as a pact with the dead and to remind the men to keep the faith—and the secret. Never show the envelope to anyone and never, ever open it. And soon—very soon now—the gold would be theirs.

It was about this time when the wives grew suspicious. They had been aware of the gatherings, of course, those secret meetings from which they had been excluded and from which their husbands would often come home drunk. But about the exchange of money for the promise of treasure, the women had been kept entirely in the dark. So when the miller's wife found the unusual envelope in her husband's pocket, she became curious. And when she opened it and found the dust, she became alarmed, believing it to be evidence of witchcraft. When she confronted her husband, he grew terrified and revealed the whole affair. His wife immediately saw the ruse and set out to reveal Rogers for the huckster that he was.

As rumor began to spread that the congregants had been duped, and a cloud of doubt descended on the town, nighttime visitations from the white-sheeted phantom suddenly became more frequent. Apparently, the Morristown Ghost was out to reaffirm their faith. But the ghost itself must have gotten frightened at this point, feeling its hold on the community loosening, because it got a bit sloppy, maybe even a little drunk. And one morning, after being visited by the ghost, one of the men found footprints outside his house, forming a trail that led him right to Rogers's door. And when he discovered the white sheet in Rogers's possession, the jig was up.

Rogers was arrested and confessed to the whole affair. He confessed to creating the explosions with his knowledge of chemistry, confessed to wearing the white sheet and gliding over the town with the aid of ropes and stilts, confessed to being in cahoots with men dressed as ghosts who rapped on walls and windows and collected coins beneath a certain tree beside a certain mountain glade. Those coins—about £500 worth—were never returned, and after posting bail, Rogers escaped and continued to con other treasure seekers from Pennsylvania to New Hampshire, far away from Morris County. And while gold was never found on Schooley's Mountain, its mineral water certainly made many healthy, if not wealthy.

As for the Morristown Ghost, the men had to admit it didn't exist. Their need to believe kept them blind to the obvious deception. And I guess there's a warning in that for us all.

CHAPTER 15

THE SPIRIT OF
THE SUSSEX SORCERER

In a clearing on the side of Sunrise Mountain, I stood on a stone in the light of the setting sun. I was thinking of all the times I used to stand in that same spot back when I was just old enough to drive. Escaping the suburbs in my mom's Cavalier, I would drive out there to hike at Stokes State Forest. And there, at the top of the Kittatinny Ridge, I would reach for the magic of the stars and feel like I could leap and leave the earth. Thirty years later, there I was, still earthbound and still reaching. But as I closed my eyes and listened to the silence, I started to float a little out of time and space... until I heard the angry sound of thrashing in the trees.

Startled, I fell off the stone and ran for the safety of the car, where I waited for the bear to appear. I mean, it had to be a bear, right? Nothing else could come crashing through the trees like that. But nothing came into the clearing. So I got out of the car, got back up on the stone and tried to get back to that peaceful place. But now one eye was open, and a question haunted my mind: What the *hell* was that?

What I didn't know then is that a bear was the least of the fearful things I might encounter on that mountain. I had heard of the ghost of the Sussex Sorcerer, but I never knew he'd been spotted where I stood. Only later, while reading Beck's *Roads of Home*, did I learn that this spirit, also known as Uncle Phillip, had been said to leave his home in nearby Frankford Township and wander around the surrounding mountains.

The spirit of the Sussex Sorcerer may surprise you as you soak up the scenic view at the top of Sunrise Mountain. *Robert Oakes.*

In telling about the Uncle Phillip tale back in 1956, Beck referenced a much older version of the story, found in *Historical Collections of the State of New Jersey* by John Barber and Henry Howe, published in 1846. Where Barber and Howe got it from, I don't know. They offer no specific source, though in their preface, they tell how they traveled the state gathering both oral and written accounts "by those who resided on the spot." Their aim was to "rescue…many incidents which attend this extraordinary age…which would otherwise be lost in the lapse of time." And indeed, the Uncle Phillip story has not been lost to time. In fact, it has appeared as recently as 2004 in *Haunted New Jersey* by Martinelli and Stansfield and again in 2006 in *Spooky New Jersey* by S.E. Schlosser. In these most recent versions of the story, we learn that Uncle Phillip, who was an eccentric recluse in life, returned after death as a ghost to avenge himself for mistreatment he'd suffered at the hands of mischievous children, making him into a kind of bogeyman figure.

But in the 1846 version of the story, there is no mention of Uncle Phillip's postmortem return. Instead, the focus is on the strangeness that pervaded his earthly existence, on his occult practices and his belief in "witchcraft, ghosts, hobgoblins, or any other creature of superstition," as well as in divination and "the art of magic." We hear about his use of a "composition stored away in his pocket" that granted him "immunity from all the spells and machinations of demons and witches" and of how he broke charms, exorcized demons and cured mysterious illnesses, all with the aid of magic.

We learn, too, about his "heavenly studies," of how he would often escape to high places to draw wisdom from the magic of the stars.

People either laughed at Uncle Phillip because of his odd behavior or they gave him a wide berth. Neighborhood children pulled pranks, sometimes stealing from him or surrounding his house at night to bang on drums and bells and then blame it all on witchery. This Uncle Phillip was only too willing to believe, as "he seemed to regard almost every person with distrust, suspecting them of being leagued with witches and evil spirits against himself." His years of mistrusting others and his "perpetual brooding over dark mysterious subjects" gave him a "wild and unnatural" appearance; he was "bent and misshapen" with a "swarthy, lantern-jawed, unshaven visage…[and] a deep-set, wild and wandering eye which seemed ever and anon looking out for specters."

And according to the more recent versions of the tale, when Uncle Phillip himself became a specter, he returned to take revenge on those who had tormented him, especially on those children whose foolish pranks paled in comparison to the dark arts of the Sussex Sorcerer, especially now that his spirit had been unleashed. After suffering through a few fearful nights of strange visions, appearances and disembodied sounds, the children begged for the ghost's forgiveness and gave up their mischievous ways.

Beck said the ghost of Uncle Phillip still walks along the Kittatinny Ridge, from Sunfish Pond to Sunrise Mountain, a "feeble wraith, bent almost double…truly a long way from home." Maybe, if you go, you might meet him there, maybe down a dark path or in a sunlit clearing. And maybe he'll surprise you with a thrashing in the trees that'll make you want to run away. But if you stay, maybe you'll find that Uncle Phillip isn't angry anymore. Maybe he just wants what he always wanted: to be left in peace up there on that mountain, all alone and reaching for the magic of the stars.

AFTERWORD

I hope you have enjoyed this exploration of the ghost lore of northwestern New Jersey. May it help awaken your love for the stories of your home, wherever that may be, and inspire you to explore the many mysteries all around us in our world. Whether or not you believe in ghosts, I think it is worthwhile to look for them, because whenever we immerse ourselves in the unseen spirit of a place, our experience becomes that much richer and more meaningful.

BIBLIOGRAPHY

Books

Armstrong, William C. *Pioneer Families of Northwestern New Jersey*. Baltimore, MD: Clearfield, 2002.

Banta, Theodore M. *Sayre Family: Lineage of Thomas Sayre*. New York: De Vinne Press, 1901.

Barber, John W., and Henry Howe. *Historical Collections of the State of New Jersey*. New York: S. Tuttle, 1846.

Beck, Henry Charlton. *The Roads of Home: Lanes and Legends of New Jersey*. New Brunswick, NJ: Rutgers University Press, 1987.

———. *Tales and Towns of Northern New Jersey*. New Brunswick, NJ: Rutgers University Press, 1988.

Brodhead, L.W. *The Delaware Water Gap: Its Legends and Early History*. Philadelphia: Sherman & Co. Printers, 1870.

Cohen, David Steven. *Folklore and Folklife of New Jersey*. New Brunswick, NJ: Rutgers University Press, 1983.

———. *Folk Legacies Revisited*. New Brunswick, NJ: Rutgers University Press, 1995.

Cunningham, John T. *The New Jersey Sampler: Historic Tales of Old New Jersey*. Upper Montclair, NJ: N.J. Almanac, 1964.

———. *This Is New Jersey*. New Brunswick, NJ: Rutgers University Press, 1994.

Dalton, Richard F., et al. *Caves of New Jersey*. Trenton, NJ: Bureau of Geology & Topography, 1976.

Dann, Kevin T. *25 Walks in New Jersey*. New Brunswick, NJ: Rutgers University Press, 1983.

Fleming, Thomas J. *New Jersey: A History*. New York: Norton, 1984.

Gillespie, Angus Kress, and Michael Aaron Rockland. *Looking for America on the New Jersey Turnpike*. New Brunswick, NJ: Rutgers University Press, 1989.

Halsey, Edmund Drake. *History of Morris County, New Jersey*. New York: W.W. Munsell, 1882.

Hauck, Dennis William. *Haunted Places: The National Directory*. New York: Penguin, 1997.

Hladik, L'Aura. *Ghosthunting New Jersey*. Cincinnati, OH: Clerisy Press, 2008.

Kobbé, Gustav. *The Central Railroad of New Jersey: An Illustrated Guide-Book*. New York: n.p., 1890.

Le Blanc, Antoine, et al. *S.P. Hull's Report of the Trial and Conviction of Antoine Le Blanc for the Murder of the Sayre Family: At Morristown, N.J., on the Night of the Eleventh of May, 1833: With His Confession, as Given to Mr. A. Boisaubin, the Interpreter*. New York: Lewis Nichols, Printer, 1833.

Lowenthal, Larry. *Iron Mine Railroads of Northern New Jersey*. Morristown, NJ: Tri-State Railway Historical Society, 1981.

Lurie, Maxine N., and Marc Mappen, eds. *Encyclopedia of New Jersey*. New Brunswick, NJ: Rutgers University Press, 2005.

Macken, Lynda Lee. *Ghosts of the Garden State*. Forked River, NJ: Black Cat Press, 2001.

———. *Ghosts of the Garden State II*. Forked River, NJ: Black Cat Press, 2003.

———. *Ghosts of the Garden State III*. Forked River, NJ: Black Cat Press, 2005.

———. *Haunted Houses of New Jersey: History and Mystery in the Garden State*. Forked River, NJ: Black Cat Press, 2016.

Mappen, Marc. *Jerseyana: The Underside of New Jersey History*. New Brunswick, NJ: Rutgers University Press, 1992.

———. *There's More to New Jersey Than the Sopranos*. New Brunswick, NJ: Rivergate Books, 2009.

Martinelli, Patricia A., and Charles A. Stansfield. *The Big Book of New Jersey Ghost Stories*. Mechanicsburg, PA: Stackpole Books, 2013.

———. *Haunted New Jersey: Ghosts and Strange Phenomena of the Garden State*. Mechanicsburg, PA: Stackpole Books, 2004.

McCloy, James F., and Ray Miller. *The Jersey Devil*. Wilmington, DE: Middle Atlantic Press, 1976.

Moran, Mark, and Mark Sceurman. *Weird N.J.: Your Travel Guide to New Jersey's Local Legends and Best Kept Secrets, Vol. 1*. New York: Sterling Publishing, 2005.

———. *Weird N.J.: Your Travel Guide to New Jersey's Local Legends and Best Kept Secrets, Vol. 2*. New York: Sterling Publishing, 2006.

———. *Weird N.J. Presents: Home State Hauntings: True Stories of Ghostly Places in New Jersey*. Weird NJ, 2013.

Myers, Arthur. *The Ghostly Register: Haunted Dwellings, Active Spirits: A Journey to America's Strangest Landmarks*. Chicago: Contemporary Books, 1986.

The Original History of the Morristown Ghost, a Fac-Simile Copy. Morristown, NJ: 1876.

Quarrie, George. *Within a Jersey Circle: Tales of the Past, Grave and Gay, As Picked Up from Old Jerseyites*. Somerville, NJ: Unionist-Gazette Association Publishers, 1910.

Roberts, Russell. *Discover the Hidden New Jersey*. New Brunswick, NJ: Rutgers University Press, 1995.

Rosenfeld, Lucy D., and Marina Harrison. *History Walks in New Jersey: Exploring the Heritage of the Garden State*. New Brunswick, NJ: Rivergate Books, 2006.

Sarapin, Janice Kohl. *Old Burial Grounds of New Jersey: A Guide*. New Brunswick, NJ: Rutgers University Press, 1994.

Schlosser, S.E. *Spooky New Jersey: Tales of Hauntings, Strange Happenings, and Other Local Lore*. Guilford, CT: Insiders' Guide, 2006.

Schrabisch, Max. *Indian Habitations in Sussex County, New Jersey*. Union Hill, NJ: Dispatch Printing Company, 1915.

Sherman, Andrew M. *Historic Morristown, New Jersey: The Story of Its First Century*. Morristown, NJ: Howard Publishing, 1905.

Smyk, Edward A. *Historic Passaic County: An Illustrated History*. San Antonio, TX: Historical Publishing Network, 2004.

Snell, James P., and W. W. Clayton. *History of Sussex and Warren Counties, New Jersey: With Illustrations and Biographical Sketches of Its Prominent Men and Pioneers*. Philadelphia: Everts and Peck, 1881.

Stockton, Frank R. *Stories of New Jersey*. New York: American Book Company, 1896.

Tales of New Jersey: Being a Collection of the Best Tales, Fact and Folklore That Have Appeared in the Pages of Tel-News, the Informal Publication Sent to All New Jersey Bell Customers Since 1935. New Jersey Bell Telephone Co., 1963.

Wagner, Eleanor. *Sussex County Hauntings and Other Strange Phenomena, Part 1.* N.p., 2019.

———. *Sussex County Hauntings and Other Strange Phenomena, Part 2.* N.p., 2020.

Wharton, Edith. *The Ghost Stories of Edith Wharton.* New York: Simon & Schuster, 1997.

Zimmerman, Linda. *Ghost Investigator, Vol. 4: Ghosts of New York and New Jersey.* Blooming Grove, NY: Spirited Books, 2004.

Zwillenberg, Elias. *New Jersey Haunts.* Atglen, PA: Schiffer Publishing, 2010.

Print Articles

Ambroz, Jillian Hornbeck. "At the Stanhope House, Echoes of Past and Beat of Present." *New York Times,* October 22, 2000.

Augustine, William F. "The Roots of Waterloo Village." *Star Ledger* (Newark, NJ), 1950.

Barron, James. "An 'Explorer' Investigates State Caves." *New York Times,* August 28, 1977.

Beck, Henry Charlton. "Ruins at Frenche's Pond Mark Site of Mysterious Venture." *Star Ledger* (Newark, NJ), July 25, 1954.

———. "Waterloo's Thriving Past Hidden in New Growth Trees." *Star Ledger* (Newark, NJ), September 5, 1954.

Carlson, Cristy. "The Newton Fire Museum: Renovations, Ghosts and History." *New Jersey Herald* (Newton, NJ), October 4, 2018.

Chatham (NJ) Press. "Step Back in Time to Waterloo Village." June 14, 1979.

Chesler, Caren. "The Longest Light." *New York Times,* June 24, 2001.

Democrat and Chronicle. "Antics of a New Jersey Spook." January 4, 1886.

Galena (KS) Weekly Republican. "A Spy's Stratagem: How a British Officer Secured Information of Washington's Army." October 29, 1892.

Greensboro Daily News. "Descendants of White Pilgrim Gather to Honor His Memory." August 22, 1914.

Hanley, Robert. "Body of Jersey Scoutmaster Is Recovered from the Cave." *New York Times,* March 31, 1982.

Hazleton (PA) Sentinel. "The Hero of Moody's Cave." April 30, 1896.

James, George. "No Rest for the Eerie." *New York Times,* October 26, 1997.

Jersey City (NJ) News. "A Four Days' Outing: Story of the Trip of Two Gentlemen Among the Jersey Mountains." July 24, 1894.

Kurczewski, Nick. "Clinton Road, New Jersey: The Scariest and Strangest Road in the U.S." *New York Daily News,* October 2, 2019.

Leon, Brian. "Haunted Halloween Road Trips: Shades of Death Road, Warren County, New Jersey." *New York Daily News*, October 2, 2019.

MacNutt, W.S. "The Narrative of Lieutenant James Moody." *Acadiensis: Journal of the History of the Atlantic Region* 1, no. 2 (1972): 72–90.

Madison Eagle (Madison, NJ). "Scouts Hope to Revive Activities Which Once Stirred Frenche's Folly." May 7, 1946.

Mappen, Marc. "Jerseyana." *New York Times*, October 13, 1991.

New Jersey Herald (Newton, NJ). "Church Members Welcomed Home at Yellow Frame." June 14, 2012.

———. "Mischief-Making 'Ghost' Prowls Fire Museum." September 13, 2011.

———. "Sussex County Once Had an Underground Railroad." May 1, 2016.

New York Times. "Lake Hopatcong." August 21, 1874.

Passaic (NJ) Daily News. "Lackawanna's Big Cutoff Completed." December 19, 1911.

Prugh, Byron M., ed. "The Haunted House." *Lake Hopatcong (NJ) Breeze*, July 10, 1909.

Republican (Darlington, WI). "The Morristown Ghost." January 4, 1878.

Taylor, A. Van Doren, editor. "Lake Hopatcong's Sea Serpent." *Angler* (Lake Hopatcong, NJ), August 4, 1894.

Taylor, Alan. "The Early Republic's Supernatural Economy: Treasure Seeking in the American Northeast, 1780–1830." *American Quarterly* 38, no. 1 (1986): 6–34.

Twice-a-Week Dispatch (Burlington, NC). "Thomas Reunion Is Held." August 28, 1914.

Tuttle, Joseph F. "The Morristown Ghost." *Historical Magazine*, January 1872.

Whiteman, Lew. "When Greene County Sheltered 'The White Pilgrim.'" *Dayton (OH) Daily News*, February 20, 1921.

World (New York, NY). "It Must Be a Ghost." January 15, 1894.

———. "Nelly Bly and the Ghost." February 4, 1894.

Yarrow, Andrew L. "Music and History at Waterloo Village." *New York Times*, June 17, 1988.

Online Articles and Blog Posts

Advertiser-News North (Andover, NJ). "Ghost Hunting Is Alive and Well in Sussex County." www.advertisernewsnorth.com/news/ghost-hunting-is-alive-and-well-in-sussex-county-XDAN20101222312229977.

Affordable Colleges Online. "13 Most Haunted College Campuses." July 27, 2021. www.affordablecollegesonline.org/college-resource-center/13-most-haunt-college-campuses.

Alder, Jeremy. "Top 10 Most Haunted Colleges in America." College Consensus. November 29, 2021. https://www.collegeconsensus.com/rankings/most-haunted-colleges/.

Amberdm. "Shades of Death Road." Scary Urban Legends, https://www.wattpad.com/45720150-scary-urban-legends-shades-of-death-road.

America's Most Haunted. "Clinton Road—America's Most Haunted Roadway." February 1, 2016. www.americas-most-haunted.com/2016/02/01/clinton-road-americas-most-haunted-roadway.

American Folklore. "Turnabout Is Fairplay." americanfolklore.net/folklore/2011/07/turnabout_is_fairplay.html.

Andover New Jersey Historic Sites. "Revolutionary War Sites in Andover, New Jersey." www.revolutionarywarnewjersey.com/new_jersey_revolutionary_war_sites/towns/andover_nj_revolutionary_war_sites.htm.

Ash, Lorraine. "Got Ghosts? Tour These Haunted Houses." *Morristown (NJ) Daily Record*, October 7, 2015, www.dailyrecord.com/story/news/2015/10/07/got-ghosts-tour-these-haunted-houses/73411498/.

Atlas Obscura. "Jenny Jump State Forest." January 20, 2015. www.atlasobscura.com/places/jenny-jump-state-forest.

Bergstein, Dan. "Haunted NJ: Clinton Road." Best of NJ. March 21, 2019. bestofnj.com/features/holidays/halloween/haunted-nj-clinton-road.

Bob Dylan's Musical Roots. "The Lone Pilgrim (Trad./Elder John Ellis)." bobdylanroots.com/lone.html.

Brodesser-Akner, Taffy. "The Most Haunted Road in America." Atlas Obscura. May 12, 2016. longreads.com/2015/10/27/the-most-haunted-road-in-america.

Burkhart, Roberta. "Mystery at the Manse." New Jersey Hills. May 28, 2015, www.newjerseyhills.com/entertainment/mystery-at-the-manse/article_11950a26-b33f-564d-a9f8-8a5a6fc28c84.html.

Byrd, Deborah. "Ghost Lights: Believe If You Dare: Human World." EarthSky. October 30, 2016. earthsky.org/human-world/ghost-lights-believe-in-them-if-you-dare.

Calliope's Corner. "The Legend of Hookerman." calliopescorner.weebly.com/the-legend-of-hookerman.html.

Carroll, Peggy. "The Morristown Ghost (or: Beware of Ghosts Promising Gifts)." Morristown Green, March 8 2017, morristowngreen.com/2016/10/27/the-morristown-ghost-or-beware-of-ghosts-promising-gifts.

Coughlin, Kevin. "Ghost-Hunting? Take a Peek at Fosterfields in Morris Township." Morristown Green, July 1 2014, morristowngreen.com/2014/07/01/ghost-hunting-take-a-peek-at-fosterfields-in-morris-township.

Crespolini, Russ. "Drew University Makes Insider List of Haunted Campuses." Patch, October 31, 2019, patch.com/new-jersey/madison/drew-university-makes-insider-list-haunted-campuses.

———. "Truth or Tale: Hopatcong's 'Lakeness' Monster." Patch, October 15, 2020, patch.com/new-jersey/hopatcong-sparta/truth-or-tale-hopatcongs-lakeness-monster.

———. "Truth or Tale: Long Valley's Hookerman." Patch, October 6, 2020, patch.com/new-jersey/longvalley/truth-or-tale-long-valleys-hookerman.

Cubedz. "Do You Believe in Ghosts?" Medium, November 5, 2021, cubedz.medium.com/do-you-believe-in-ghosts-abf3aedc6f14.

Dangerous Roads. "Clinton Road in NJ Is Said to Be the Scariest Road in America." www.dangerousroads.org/north-america/usa/4371-clinton-roadusa.html.

———. "Shades of Death Road." www.dangerousroads.org/north-america/usa/4361-shades-of-death-road.html.

———. "The 19 Most Haunted Roads on Earth." www.dangerousroads.org/haunted-roads/4590-top-15-haunted-roads.html.

DeWinters, Dahlia. "Spooky New Jersey—The Legend of Clinton Road." Medium, October 3, 2017, medium.com/@dahliadewinters/spooky-new-jersey-the-legend-of-clinton-road-99202fe2cba4.

Dictionary of Canadian Biography. "Biography—Moody, James—Volume V (1801–1820)." www.biographi.ca/en/bio/moody_james_5E.html.

Dorsey, Carolyn. "Antoine Le Blanc: A Shocking Story of Murder and a Community's Revenge." Morristown Green, December 4, 2020, morristowngreen.com/2014/09/26/antoine-le-blanc-a-shocking-story-of-murder-and-a-communitys-revenge.

Doyle, Bill. "The Most Haunted Road in New Jersey." New Jersey 101.5, March 31, 2021, nj1015.com/the-most-haunted-road-in-new-jersey.

Eyesonlocal.com. "Lake Hopatcong History: 'The Haunted House.'"

Fleury, Larry. "The Spook Light: This Creepy, Glowing Orb Might Give You Nightmares." Farmers' Almanac, October 15, 2021, www.farmersalmanac.com/what-spooklight-150132.

Frassinelli, Mike. "N.J. Motorists Continue to Be Frustrated by 'Nation's Longest Traffic Light' on Route 23 in West Milford." NJ.com, June 14, 2010, www.nj.com/news/2010/06/nj_motorists_continue_to_be_fr.html.

Fredon New Jersey Historic Sites. "Revolutionary War Sites in Fredon, New Jersey." www.revolutionarywarnewjersey.com/new_jersey_revolutionary_war_sites/towns/fredon_nj_revolutionary_war_sites.htm.

FrightFind. "Haunted Clinton Road, America's Most Cursed Highway." September 6, 2021, frightfind.com/haunted-clinton-road.

Gaffney, Kyle. "James Moody: American Soldier." Strategy Bridge, January 6, 2017, thestrategybridge.org/the-bridge/2017/1/6/james-moody-american-soldier.

Genader, Ann. "Cross Castle Is Gone Forever, but the Memories Remain." NorthJersey.com, August 10, 2018, www.northjersey.com/story/news/passaic/west-milford/2018/08/10/cross-castle-newfoundland-gone-forever-but-memories-remain/948442002.

Genovese, Peter. "N.J.'s 10 Creepiest Places: Don't Read This List If You Scare Easily!" NJ.com, October 29, 2014, www.nj.com/entertainment/2014/10/njs_10_creepiest_places_-_dont_read_this_list_if_you_scare_easily.html.

Geocaching. "Moody's Rock." www.geocaching.com/geocache/GC1M3GR_moodys-rock?guid=cc79fc70-6bdc-453f-9c66-68218cd80a3d.

———. "Nariticong Clan Tribute." www.geocaching.com/geocache/GC2QA45_nariticong-clan-tribute?guid=1563fc3e-b98e-45de-90f1-9a4e2a8ecd00.

Ghost Hosts, Drew University. "Ghost Hosts." haunteddrew.com.

Griffith, Janelle. "'Paranormal Evenings' in Morristown Offers a Ghoulishly Good Time." NJ.com, August 2, 2014, www.nj.com/entertainment/2014/08/ghost_hunting_morristown.html.

Grundhauser, Eric. "Shades of Death Road." Atlas Obscura, October 24, 2014, www.atlasobscura.com/places/shades-of-death-road.

Hackettstown LiFE. "The Hooker Man Long Valley." www.hackettstownlife.com/forum/719138.

Harp, Scott. "Joseph Thomas: The White Pilgrim." History of the Restoration Movement, www.therestorationmovement.com/_states/nj/thomas.htm.

Haunted Hovel. "Haunted Places in New Jersey." www.hauntedhovel.com/hauntedplacesinnewjersey.html.

Haunted Rooms America. "The Most Haunted Places in New Jersey." December 16, 2021, www.hauntedrooms.com/new-jersey/haunted-places.

Heaney, Katie. "6 Scary Things I Saw on the Most Haunted Road in America." BuzzFeed, August 17, 2020, www.buzzfeed.com/katieheaney/6-scary-things-i-saw-on-the-most-haunted-road-in-america.

Hidden New Jersey. "Forging Iron, Not Fright, on Clinton Road." www.
   hiddennj.com/2014/06/forging-iron-not-fright-on-clinton-road.html.
———. "Long Pond Ironworks: Walking through a Century in an Hour
   or So." www.hiddennj.com/2011/07/long-pond-ironworks-walking-
   through.html.
Historical Marker Database. "The Gorge Bridge Train Wreck Historical
   Marker." June 16, 2016, www.hmdb.org/m.asp?m=21806.
———. "Clinton Ironworks Historical Marker." June 16, 2016, www.
   hmdb.org/m.asp?m=35062.
Hushed Up History. "The Lingering Leather of Antoine Le Blanc."
   husheduphistory.tumblr.com/post/190358533028/.
Hymnary.org. "I Came to the Place Where the Lone Pilgrim Lay."
   hymnary.org/text/i_came_to_the_place_where_the_lone_pilgr.
Hymntime.com. "The White Pilgrim." www.hymntime.com/tch/htm/w/
   h/i/t/whitpilg.htm.
Iapoce, Connor. "Take a Road Trip through N.J.'s Spooky Ghost Towns
   to See Peculiar Pieces of History." Jersey's Best, October 1, 2021, www.
   jerseysbest.com/community/take-a-road-trip-through-n-j-s-spooky-
   ghost-towns-to-see-peculiar-pieces-of-history.
Investigations into the Unknown and Weird. "Shades of Death Road."
   silentthrill.wordpress.com/tag/old-mine-road.
IvyWise. "5 Of the Most Haunted College Campuses." October 8, 2020,
   www.ivywise.com/blog/5-of-the-most-haunted-college-campuses.
Izzo, Michael. "Expert: Lake Hopatcong Boa Is Green Anaconda."
   Daily Record, July 23, 2014, www.dailyrecord.com/story/
   news/local/2014/07/18/expert-lake-hopatcong-boa-green-
   anaconda/12859459.
———. "Lake Hopatcong's Original Sea Creature." NorthJersey.com, July
   19, 2014, www.northjersey.com/story/news/local/2014/07/19/lake-
   hopatcongs-original-sea-creature/12846533.
Jennings, Rob. "This N.J. Rail Bridge Is Beloved by Many, but Nobody
   Knows What to Do with It." Nj.com, January 13, 2020, www.nj.com/
   news/2019/11/this-nj-rail-bridge-is-beloved-by-many-but-nobody-
   knows-what-to-do-with-it.html.
Jones, Benji. "The Swamp Science That Lured Travelers to Their Doom
   and Inspired the Jack-o'-Lantern." Popular Science, April 26, 2021,
   www.popsci.com/jack-o-lanterns-marsh-lights.
Joplin Missouri. "The Spook Light: Joplin, MO." www.joplinmo.org/575/
   The-Spook-Light#:~:text=Others%20say%20the%20Spook%20
   Light,to%20be%20seen%20inside%20vehicles.

Koppenhaver, Bob. "Daytrip through the Pequest Valley in New Jersey."
  Skylands Visitor Magazine, www.njskylands.com/tn_pequestvalley_103.
———. "The Andover Mine in New Jersey." Skylands Visitor Magazine,
  njskylands.com/hs_mine_andover_082.
Koppenhaver, Robert. "Legendary Rocks and Boulders in New Jersey."
  Skylands Visitor Magazine, njskylands.com/tour-rocks-and-boulders.
Kumar, Suchitha. "Welcome to Clinton Road, New Jersey's Most Haunted
  Motorway." Odyssey Online, October 15, 2019, www.theodysseyonline.
  com/clinton-road-haunted-new-jersey.
Kuperinsky, Amy. "Paranormal New Jersey: Ghost Hunters
  Espouse 'Paraunity.'" NJ.com, May 29, 2014, www.nj.com/
  entertainment/2014/05/new_jersey_paraunity_expo_new_jersey_
  paranormal_ghost_hunters.html.
———. "The 8 Most Historic (Real) Haunted Houses in N.J." NJ.com,
  October 30, 2016, www.nj.com/entertainment/2016/10/historic_
  haunted_houses_nj.html.
———. "The Legend of N.J.'s Clinton Road Inspires Movie with
  Ice-T, Vincent Pastore." NJ.com, June 13, 2019, www.nj.com/
  entertainment/2019/06/watch-the-legend-of-njs-clinton-road-inspires-
  movie-with-ice-t-vincent-pastore-heres-how-to-see-it.html.
LaMuraglia, Brian. "The Haunting of Morristown's Ford Mansion."
  Morristown Green, October 19, 2016, morristowngreen.
  com/2016/10/19/the-haunting-of-morristowns-ford-mansion.
Launch Knowledge. "Clinton Road New Jersey Facts and Myths." May 12,
  2018, www.launchknowledge.com/clinton-road-new-jersey-facts-and-
  myths.
Lehighvalleylive.com. "No Excuse for Viaduct Trespassers." January 9,
  2016, www.lehighvalleylive.com/opinion/2016/01/no_excuse_for_
  viaduct_trespass.html.
Lost Destinations. "Lost Destinations: Paulinskill Viaduct," http://www.
  lostdestinations.com/paulin.htm.
The Lostinjersey Blog. "Paulinskill Viaduct Photos." August 2, 2013,
  lostinjersey.wordpress.com/2009/04/07/paulinskill-viaduct.
Lusardi, Anthony. "Commentary: The Hookerman: A Local Ghost
  Story." New Jersey Hills, October 27, 2017, www.newjerseyhills.com/
  print_only/columns/commentary-the-hookerman-a-local-ghost-story/
  article_f88bcede-9d93-57e9-aba9-cc07c879c6da.html.
McBride, Tim. "Clinton Road Fact or Fiction." Horror, vocal.media/
  horror/clinton-road-fact-or-fiction.

McFadden, Casper. "The Haunted: Clinton Road." Morbid Library, September 13, 2020, themorbidlibrary.com/2020/07/26/the-haunted-clinton-road.

McGreevy, Y. "Ghost Talk at the Ford Mansion in Morristown." Patch, August 24, 2016, patch.com/new-jersey/morristown/ghost-talk-ford-mansion-morristown.

McLeod, Jaime. "Ghost Lights: A Weather Folklore." Farmers' Almanac, June 21, 2021, www.farmersalmanac.com/weather-ology-special-ghost-lights-14442.

Memory. "Things That Go Bump in the Night...and Then Steal Your Money." Ohio Memory, November 1, 2013, ohiomemory.ohiohistory.org/archives/1427.

Mindat.org. "Andover Iron Mine, Andover Township, Sussex." www.mindat.org/loc-12281.html.

Moriarty, Katie. "Top 5 Scariest Places in Warren County." WRNJ Radio, November 20, 2019, wrnjradio.com/top-5-scariest-places-in-warren-county.

Morris County Park Commission. "Paranormal Evenings Come to Fosterfields Speedwell on Saturday, May 4." www.morrisparks.net/index.php/info-center/press-releases/paranormal-evenings-comes-to-fosterfields-speedwell-on-saturday-may-4.

———. "Columbia Trail, Long Valley NJ." www.morrisparks.net/index.php/parks/columbia-trail.

Morristown National Historical Park Museum and Library. "Ghostly Revelations of the Ford Mansion." October 27, 2015, morristownnhpmuseum.blogspot.com/2015/10/ghostly-revelations-of-ford-mansion.html.

Muller, L'Aura. "The Haunted Restaurant of Morristown." Cromwell Hills On-Line, cromwellcrew.com/WedgewoodInn.html.

Murder by Gaslight. "Antoine Le Blanc." www.murderbygaslight.com/2010/09/antoine-le-blanc.html.

National Park Service. "Ford Mansion." www.nps.gov/morr/learn/historyculture/ford-mansion-washington-s-headquarters.htm.

New Jersey Chamber of Commerce. "Clinton Road." njchamber.com/clintonroad.

New Jersey Hills. "Help Find the Ghosts at the Historic Vail House." October 23, 2018, www.newjerseyhills.com/entertainment/help-find-the-ghosts-at-the-historic-vail-house/article_08ec52de-b6e4-564d-8703-dc6d322af296.html.

New Jersey Leisure Guide. "Waterloo Village: A Visitors Guide." www.new-jersey-leisure-guide.com/waterloo-village.html.

New Jersey Monthly. "13 Haunting Ghost Tales and Trails." September 27, 2016, njmonthly.com/articles/arts-entertainment/13-haunting-ghost-tales-and-trails.

News 12—New Jersey. "Looking for a Road Trip? Check out Waterloo Village in Allamuchy Mountain State Park." https://newjersey.news12.com/looking-for-a-road-trip-check-out-waterloo-village-in-allamuchy-mountain-state-park.

94.5 PST. "Why Is Clinton Road New Jersey's Most Haunted Road?" October 25, 2018, wpst.com/why-is-clinton-road-new-jerseys-most-haunted-road.

NJ.gov. "Map Archive of New Jersey's Abandoned Mines." New Jersey Geological and Water Survey, New Jersey Department of Environmental Protection. www.state.nj.us/dep/njgs/enviroed/minemaps.htm.

NJ Hiking. "Columbia Trail." July 3, 2021, www.njhiking.com/columbia-trail/.

———. "Schooley's Mountain." June 29, 2021, www.njhiking.com/schooleys-mountain/.

NJskylands.com. "The Personality of Northwest New Jersey Skylands." njskylands.com.

Novak, Steve. "How Every Warren County Town Got Its Name (And How Their Borders Changed More Than You Think)." Lehighvalleylive.com, June 28, 2018, www.lehighvalleylive.com/warren-county/2018/06/warren_county_town_names.html.

O'Neill, James M. "Morris Canal: A Century after Its Demise, 102-Mile Watery Relic Is Reborn with New Role." Northjersey.com, www.northjersey.com/story/news/environment/2017/11/26/morris-canal-century-after-its-demise-102-mile-watery-relic-reborn-new-role/418716001.

Online Bachelor Degrees. "50 Most Haunted Universities and Colleges around the World." January 20, 2022, www.online-bachelor-degrees.com/50-most-haunted-schools-around-the-world/#28-drew-university.

Online Schools Center. "50 Most Haunted Colleges and Campuses." August 3, 2021, www.onlineschoolscenter.com/50-haunted-colleges-campuses.

Only In Your State. "Driving Down This Haunted New Jersey Road Will Give You Nightmares." April 25, 2016, www.onlyinyourstate.com/new-jersey/nj-haunted-shades-of-death.

———. "The Mysterious North Carolina Legend That's Terrified Generation after Generation." November 7, 2016, www.onlyinyourstate.com/north-carolina/joe-baldwin-maco-light-nc.

————. "Stay Away from New Jersey's Most Haunted Street after Dark or You May Be Sorry." March 3, 2021, www.onlyinyourstate.com/new-jersey/avoid-clinton-road-nj-after-dark.

————. "This Abandoned New Jersey Bridge Was Once Known as the Eighth Wonder of the World." July 8, 2019, www.onlyinyourstate.com/new-jersey/amazing-abandoned-bridge-nj.

Outta the Way! "Paulinskill Viaduct Hainesburg, New Jersey." November 11, 2011, outtaway.blogspot.com/2011/11/paulinskill-viaduct.html.

Painter, Sally. "10 Haunted Universities from Coast to Coast." LoveToKnow, September 1, 2021, paranormal.lovetoknow.com/ghosts-hauntings/10-most-haunted-colleges.

Paranormal. "Clinton Road, New Jersey, United States." Amino, December 16, 2017, aminoapps.com/c/paranormal/page/blog/clinton-road-new-jersey-united-states/06wE_eNnhkuQNzPvVbW0rL5b104lxZ2zJ5p.

Paranormal & Ghost Society. "Waterloo Village." www.paranormalghostsociety.org/Waterloo.asp.

Pennsylvania Haunts & History (blog). "Dark and Stormy Drew." 2009. hauntsandhistory.blogspot.com/2009/08/dark-and-stormy-drew.html.

————. "The Legend of the Spirit Lodge." 2010. hauntsandhistory.blogspot.com/2010/05/legend-of-spirit-lodge.html.

Philippart, Tia. "America's Most Haunted Roads and Their Terrifying Legends." Impulsive Wanderlust, October 14, 2019, www.impulsivewanderlust.com/americas-haunted-roads-and-their-legends.

Pie Time. "Clinton Road: The Most Haunted Highway in the United States." March 10, 2017, buttoncoates.tumblr.com/post/158204408971/clinton-road-the-most-haunted-highway-in-the.

Presinzano, Jessica. "Stranger Jersey: Clinton Road and Dead Man's Curve." NorthJersey.com, October 29, 2018, www.northjersey.com/story/entertainment/2017/10/17/Clinton-road-and-dead-mans-curve-stranger-jersey/773080001.

————. "Stranger Jersey: The Monster of Lake Hopatcong." NorthJersey.com, October 29, 2018, www.northjersey.com/story/entertainment/2018/10/29/stranger-jersey-sea-serpent-lake-hopatcong-nj/1805341002.

Racing Nellie Bly. "Nellie Bly Articles Provided Powerful Ammunition in Pulitzer's Battle for Readers." May 7, 2017, racingnelliebly.com/strange_times/nellie-bly-articles-provided-ammunition-in-pulitzers-battle-for-readers.

Reyes, Katherine. "A Trip to Clinton Road: The Scariest Road in New Jersey." *Gothic Times* (Jersey City, NJ), gothictimes.net/7804/features/a-trip-to-clinton-road-the-scariest-road-in-new-jersey.

RoadsideAmerica.com. "Stanhope, NJ: Waterloo Village: Ghost Town." www.roadsideamerica.com/tip/53001.

Roadtrippers. "Are You Brave Enough to Drive Down the Most Haunted Road in America?" maps.roadtrippers.com/trips/15740010.

———. "Clinton Road." maps.roadtrippers.com/us/west-milford-nj/attractions/clinton-road.

———. "Cross Castle." maps.roadtrippers.com/us/nj/nature/cross-castle.

Rose, Lisa. "Creepy New Jersey: The Stuff of Legends." NJ.com, April 13, 2012, www.nj.com/entertainment/2012/04/creepy_new_jersey_the_stuff_of.html.

Ruse, Leslie. "Halloween at 'Historic Speedwell.'" *Morristown (NJ) Daily Record*, October 31, 2015, www.dailyrecord.com/story/life/home-garden/luxury/2015/10/31/halloween-historic-speedwell/74867518/.

Sapone, Patti. "Here Are 13 Haunted Places to Visit in New Jersey." NJ.com, October 28, 2018, nj.com/life-and-culture/erry-2018/10/6a88e3189f9871/want-to-see-a-ghost-yourself-h.html.

Scare Street. "Mysterious Clinton Road: Ghosts, Witches, & Haunted Urban Legends." June 4, 2019, scarestreet.com/clinton-road.

Sherwood, Joseph. "Clinton Road, New Jersey: The Scariest Road in America." A Little Bit Human, March 7, 2021, www.alittlebithuman.com/clinton-road-new-jersey-the-scariest-road-in-america.

Sparta Independent (Andover, NJ). "The Loyalist." www.spartaindependent.com/features/the-loyalist-AVSI20170921170929987.

Strange Company (blog). "The Morristown Ghost; or, Beware of Goblins Bearing Gifts." March 23, 2015, strangeco.blogspot.com/2015/03/the-morristown-ghost-or-beware-of.html.

Swancer, Brent. "Supernatural Strangeness at New Jersey's Most Cursed and Haunted Road." Mysterious Universe, October 6, 2020, mysteriousuniverse.org/2020/10/supernatural-strangeness-at-new-jerseys-most-cursed-and-haunted-road.

TAPinto. "Explore Ghost Hunting during Morristown's Paranormal Event; Sat. Aug. 18." www.tapinto.net/towns/morristown/sections/things-to-do-in-morristown/articles/explore-ghost-hunting-during-morristown-s-paranormal-event-sat-aug-18.

———. "Ghost Hunting Coming to Morristown's Frelinghuysen Arboretum; April 9." www.tapinto.net/towns/morristown/sections/

community-happenings/articles/ghost-hunting-coming-to-morristowns-frelinghuyse.

————. "Ghostly Revelations at the Ford Mansion in Morristown." www.tapinto.net/towns/morristown/sections/community-happenings/articles/ghostly-revelations-at-the-ford-mansion-in-morris.

————. "Drew University Civic Scholar Charity Ghost Tour." www.tapinto.net/towns/warren/sections/arts-and-entertainment/articles/drew-university-civic-scholar-charity-ghost-tour-15.

Thomas, Kayla. "The Most Haunted Colleges and Universities in New Jersey and Pennsylvania." 94.5 PST, October 15, 2020, wpst.com/the-most-haunted-colleges-and-universities-in-new-jersey-and-pennsylvania.

Tooley, Lynn. "Dark Moon Burying Ground." New Horizons Genealogy, www.newhorizonsgenealogicalservices.com/new-jersey-genealogy/warren-county/dark_moon_burying_ground_frelinghuysen_nj.htm.

Try to Scare Me. "Haunted Clinton Road: West Milford, NJ." September 5, 2017, www.trytoscare.me/legend/clinton-road-west-milford-2.

Turkus, Brandon. "Ghost Trucks, Haunted Bridge and Strange Lights Make Clinton Road the Scariest in the US." Autoblog, June 1, 2014, www.autoblog.com/2014/06/01/clinton-road-new-jersey-haunted-read-this.

Urban Legends Online. "The Tale of the Hookerman." October 7, 2011, urbanlegendsonline.com/the-tale-of-the-hookerman.

Vacant New Jersey. "Paulinskill Viaduct: Vacant New Jersey." www.vacantnewjersey.com/locations/paulinskillviaduct/main.html.

Van Antwerp, Vickie. "Spirits and Treasures of Schooley's Mountain." SouthJersey.com, www.southjersey.com/article/3129/Spirits-And-Treasures-Of-Schooleys-Mountain.

Walsh, Lara. "12 Colleges around the US That People Believe Are Haunted." Insider, September 30, 2019, www.insider.com/colleges-us-believed-to-be-haunted-ghosts.

Warnick, Ron. "Spook Light Legend Was Debunked More than 70 Years Ago." Route 66 News, December 16, 2018, www.route66news.com/2018/12/17/spook-light-legend-was-debunked-more-than-70-years-ago.

Waymarking.com. "Clinton Ironworks—West Milford, NJ." www.waymarking.com/waymarks/wm44NX_Clinton_Ironworks_West_Milford_NJ.

Webster, Audrey. "Clinton Road: America's Most Haunted Roadway." Lineup, July 4, 2019, the-line-up.com/clinton-road.

Weiser, Kathy. "Devil's Promenade & the Hornet Spook Light." Legends of America, www.legendsofamerica.com/mo-spooklight.

Wisti, Erin. "A Trip Down New Jersey's Clinton Road, Home to Ghosts, Satanists, and Hellhounds." Ranker, 19 June 2017, www.ranker.com/list/haunted-highway-clinton-road-new-jersey/erin-wisti.

Withers, Olivia. "Haunted New Jersey Road Will Be Focus of New Horror Movie, Report Says." NBC New York, August 9, 2017, www.nbcnewyork.com/news/local/ice-t-stars-in-new-horror-film-based-on-haunted-new-jersey-street/232354.

Wolfe, C.G. "Ghost Lights: The Legend of the Hookerman." Black River Ramblings, October 1, 2017, blackriverjournal.wordpress.com/2017/10/01/ghost-lights-the-legend-of-the-hookerman.

Zaremba, Justin. "Expert: Lake Hopatcong Snake an Anaconda, but I Was 'Sworn to Keep My Mouth Shut.'" NJ.com, July 18, 2014, www.nj.com/morris/2014/07/officials_not_taking_giant_lake_hopatcong_snake_seriously_resident_says.html.

———. "These 2 N.J. Colleges Are among the Most Haunted in U.S." NJ.com, October 15, 2017, www.nj.com/news/2017/10/these_2_nj_colleges_among_the_most_haunted_in_us.html.

Videos and Podcasts

Hometown Tales. "Hometown Tales: On the Trail of the Hookerman." March 29, 2008, www.youtube.com/watch?v=6zfMhtptm2Y.

———. "Hometown Tales: The Ghost Raiser of Schooley's Mountain." December 29, 2008, www.youtube.com/watch?v=DvNOjyi_6Zs.

It's History. "The Lost Central Railroad of New Jersey." January 6, 2022, www.youtube.com/watch?v=UEIeOozlb_Y.

Mobile Instinct. "Exploring the Tunnels and Passageways inside This Bridge." July 9, 2021, www.youtube.com/watch?v=muZ6StXz5o8.

My Great Challenge. A Guided Tour of Acorn Hall, NJ—Victorian Christmas." December 21, 2021, www.youtube.com/watch?v=BWH519B9a0k.

Myles, Pissi, and Sam Baxter. "College Is So Spoooooooooooky!" *My Spooky Gay Family* (podcast), October 15, 2020, www.podbean.com/ew/pb-xfczh-ef25bc.

New Jersey Outdoor Adventures. "Tour of Abandoned Waterloo Village a Restored Canal Town in Byram, New Jersey." June 12, 2015, www.youtube.com/watch?v=BaxLWxuGwUU.

New York Daily News. "A Haunted Ride along Clinton Road." October 30, 2014, www.youtube.com/watch?v=S2Ql0paKlys.

NorthJersey.com. "Stranger Jersey: Clinton Road & Dead Man's Curve." May 8, 2018, www.youtube.com/watch?v=Wj-BAFDZ1OA.

———. "Stranger Jersey: The Monster of Lake Hopatcong." October 29, 2018, www.youtube.com/watch?v=mNbdsMGrAGU.

The Proper People. "The Most Terrifying Road in America?" www.youtube.com/watch?v=2e9044gzLmo.

Smith, Talia. "'Tales from the Haunted Forest' with Dr. Matthew Beland." *Once Upon a Time: A Storytelling Podcast*, October 16, 2020.

SuperHorrorBro. "America's Most Haunted Highway—Clinton Road (Explained)." October 7, 2017, www.youtube.com/watch?v=mWmmHMreqLo.

TheUnknownCameraman. "Lenape Indian Cave at Shades of Death Road." September 25, 2013, www.youtube.com/watch?v=kpCZB-9FN8E.

Top5s. "5 Creepiest & Most Haunted Roads in the World." July 31, 2015, www.youtube.com/watch?v=Crm_YngYG9g.

Travel Channel. What Lies Beneath | Kindred Spirits Recap. March 6, 2020, www.youtube.com/watch?v=uIcxXh9hyyA.

Weird NJ. "Clinton Road—America's Scariest Road." soundcloud.com/user-764594835/clinton-road-americas-scariest-road.

White, Elaine, dir. *Haunted Highway*. Season 2, episode 5, "Shades of Death / Bridge of Doom." Aired December 17, 2013, on NBC. https://www.youtube.com/watch?v=lkrh4oy2rPo.

Websites

AllTrails. www.alltrails.com.

Drew University. www.drew.edu.

Facebook. www.facebook.com.

Find a Grave. www.findagrave.com.

Franklin Borough. www.franklinborough.org.

Frelinghuysen Township. livingplaces.com/NJ/Warren_County/Frelinghuysen_Township.html.

The Friends of Long Pond Ironworks. www.longpondironworks.org.

GhostsofAmerica.com. www.ghostsofamerica.com.

Hauntedplaces.org. www.hauntedplaces.org.

HauntWorld.com. www.forums.hauntworld.com.
History of Newton, New Jersey. www.newtonnj.net.
Morris Canal Greenway. www.morriscanalgreenway.org.
Morris County Historical Society. www.morriscountyhistory.org.
Morris County Park Commission. www.morrisparks.net.
Morris Tourism. www.morristourism.org.
Morristown & Morris Township Library. www.mmtlibrary.org.
New Jersey Haunted Houses. www.newjerseyhauntedhouses.com.
New Jersey Historical Society. www.jerseyhistory.org.
New Jersey Postal History Society. www.njpostalhistory.org.
Newspapers.com. www.newspapers.com.
Newton Fire Museum. www.newtonfiremuseum.org.
Newton, NJ—Official Website. www.newtontownhall.com.
North Jersey Highlands Historical Society. www.northjerseyhistory.org.
Pinterest. www.pinterest.com.
Quora. www.quora.com.
Reddit. www.reddit.com.
Stanhope House. www.stanhopehousenj.com.
Sussex County Historical Society. www.sussexhistory.org.
Twitter. www.twitter.com.
Weird NJ. www.weirdnj.com.
Wikipedia. www.wikipedia.org.
The Yellow Frame Church. www.yellowframechurch.com.

INDEX

Y

Z

ABOUT THE AUTHOR

Robert Oakes is a writer, teacher, storyteller and songwriter originally from northern New Jersey and currently residing in Western Massachusetts. In 2020, Robert's debut book, *Ghosts of the Berkshires*, was published by Arcadia Publishing. For more than a decade, Robert has led the ghost tours at Edith Wharton's the Mount in Lenox, Massachusetts, and has represented the museum and its ghosts on Syfy's *Ghost Hunters*, Jeff Belanger's *New England Legends* series on PBS and the *Apple Seed* show on BYUradio. In 2021, Robert also began leading ghost tours at Ventfort Hall and the Church on the Hill, both in Lenox, and has offered readings and presentations at museums, libraries and other venues. Robert has written and produced content for North Jersey Newspapers, AAA North Jersey, Canyon Ranch and a number of other organizations and has also taught elementary, middle and high school English.

Visit us at
www.historypress.com